DAILY DIARY
Tuesday Oct 10
Today I found a LETTER washed up in a Bottle!! I was in a hurry to open it a [read?] its content

Dear Adventurer,

We are happy you have joined us in the beginning of our exploration of **OUR EARTH: THE WATER PLANET**. Your excited puppet pals—crab, scallop, and sea star—will join you as you trek through earthquakes, volcanoes, and the ever-changing ocean floor. There are adventures on every page awaiting your discovery!

OUR EARTH books are full of intriguing science facts and experiments for you to do. You will find puzzles, mind-teasers and other activities to enjoy as you learn about the earth and plants and animals that live here.

Look for other **OUR EARTH: THE WATER PLANET** books to explore specific communities such as estuaries, coral reefs, or tidal pools that exist in the oceans of our water planet. We hope you have fun and will join us again!

Smooth sailing, Adventurer!

Your pals,

Debbie, Susan and Sailor Jack

Authors
Debra Sorrells Dixon
Susan Vaughan Henry

Illustrations
Jack Williams

Technical Editor
Lundie Spence, Ph.D.

Puppet Design
Debra Sorrells Dixon

Art Director
Susan K. Heartwell

Special Consultant
Christine San José, Ph.D.

●●●

Copyright © 1992 Puppetools, Inc.

First Edition
First Printing—1992

All rights reserved. No part of this book shall be reproduced, stored in a retrieval system, or transmitted by any means, electronic, mechanical, photocopying, recording, or otherwise, without written permission from the publisher. **Puppetools** and **Paper Talker** are registered trademarks of Prescott, Durrell & Company. The Paper Talker® puppets in this package are made available under US Patent 4,555,236. The puppets and games contained herein may be used only for individual or classroom use.

International Standard Book Number: 0-9609506-2-1
Library of Congress Catalog Card Number: 92-62163

Printed in the United States of America

OUR EARTH: THE WATER PLANET

AN INTRODUCTION

OCEANS & CONTINENTS

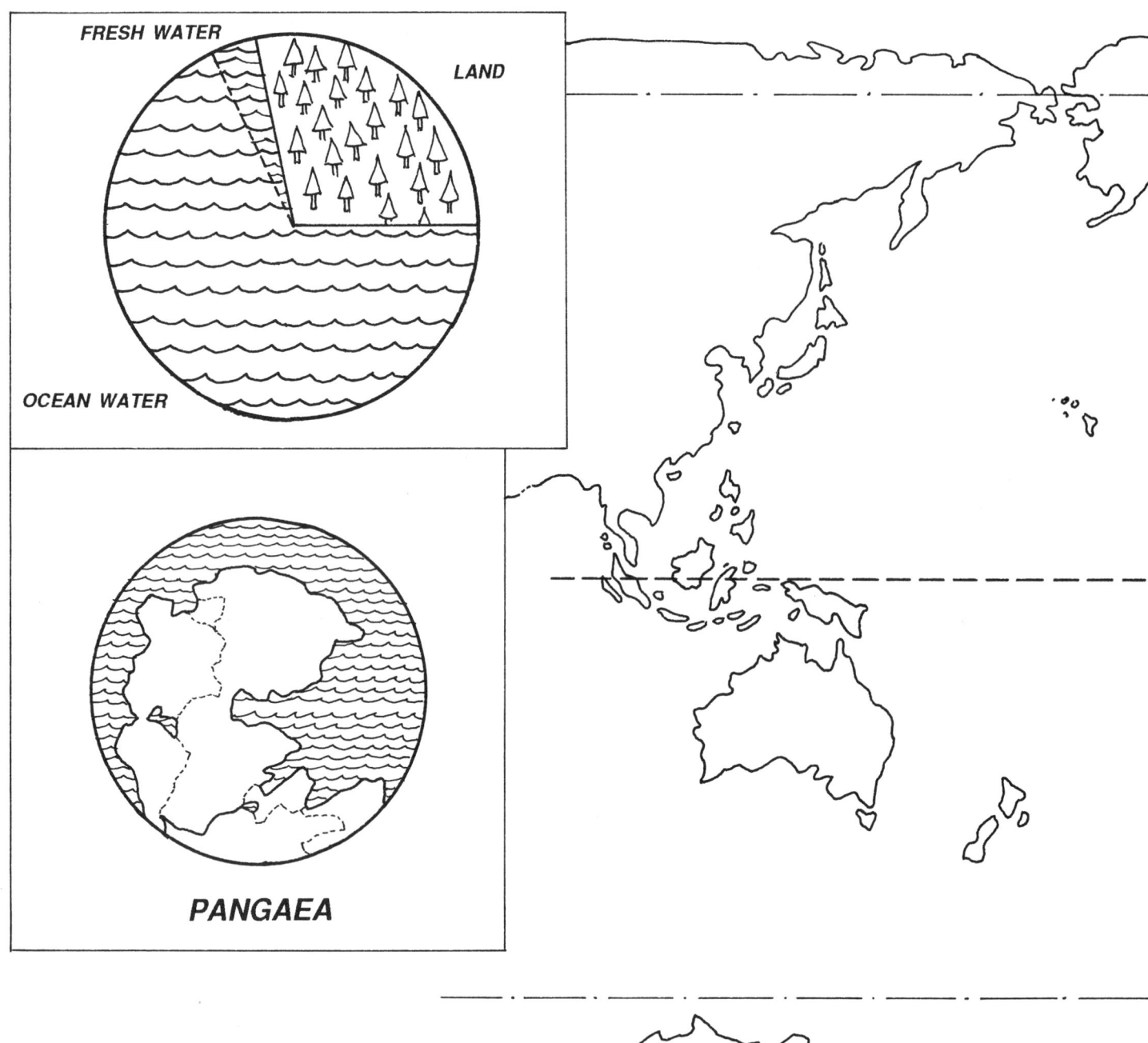

PANGAEA

Earth is the only known water planet, with over 70% of its surface covered by water. Ninety-seven per cent (97%) of all the water is seawater! All the oceans of the earth are actually one body of water, with land masses rising above the surface as continents and islands.

Meteorologists, geologists, and paleontologists have gathered evidence that over 200 million years ago, the continents were joined together as one land mass, **Pangaea**. Pangaea was surrounded by what is now the Pacific Ocean. The theory of **continental drift** proposes that the continents have been drifting apart at the rate of one inch per year.

According to the continental drift theory, which new ocean came into being when Pangaea split from north to south?

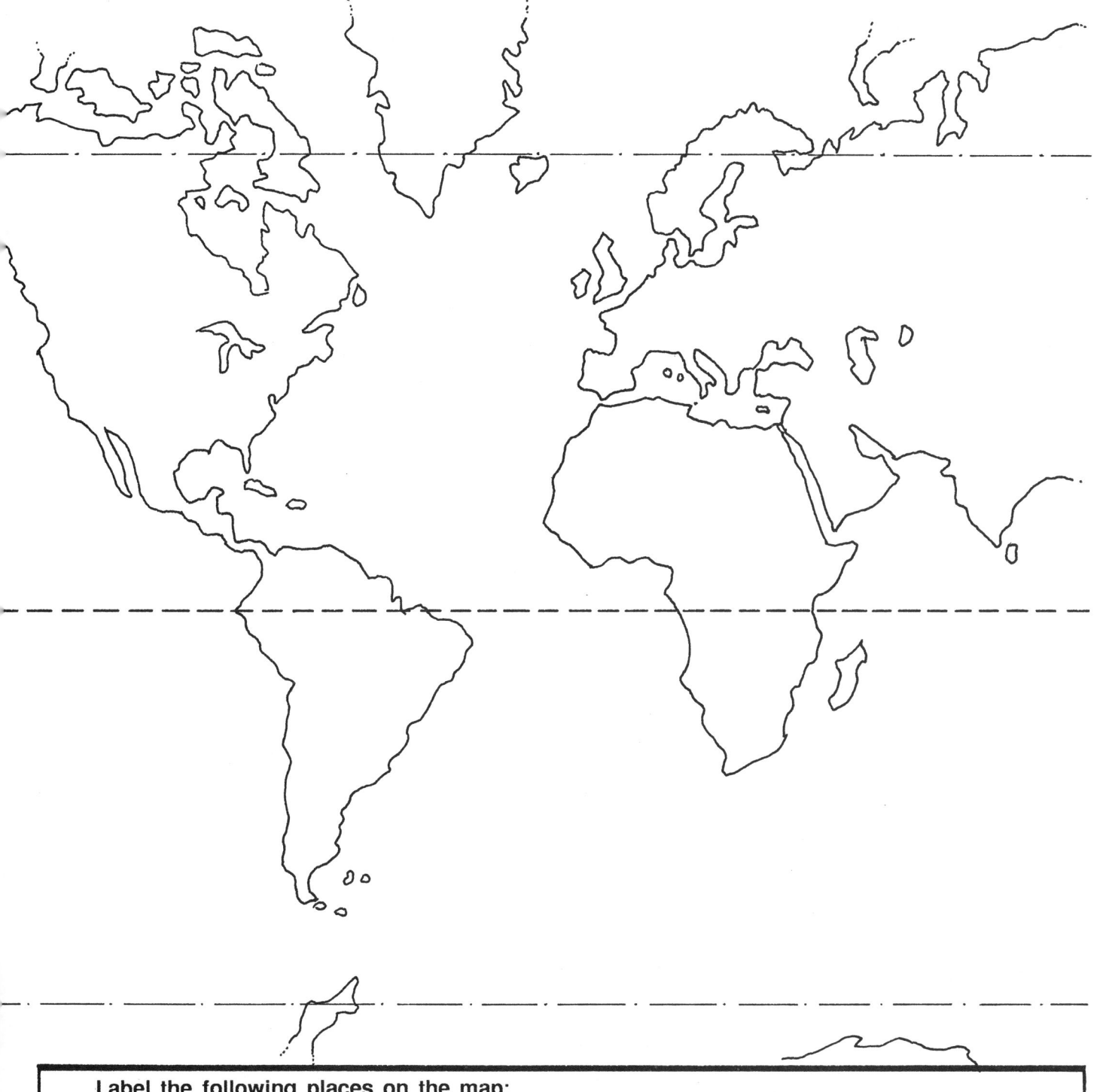

Label the following places on the map:
1. Pacific Ocean
2. Atlantic Ocean
3. Arctic Ocean
4. Antarctic Ocean
5. Indian Ocean
6. Asia
7. South America
8. North America
9. Europe
10. Africa
11. Antarctica
12. Australia

Trace the continents on a piece of paper and cut them out. How do they fit together? Can you make the pieces in the puzzle fit together to look similar to how Pangaea may have looked?

If the continental drift theory is correct, predict where the continents will be in another 200 million years. Draw a world map showing your predictions. You can invent new names for the oceans and land masses.

PLATE TECTONICS---EARTHQUAKES & VOLCANOES

According to the theory of **plate tectonics**, the earth's crust and upper part of the mantle are divided into about 20 rigid plates, which actually float on the molten material in the lower part of the **mantle**. The heat from the extremely hot core causes **convection currents** in the mantle which move the plates. *The continents ride along on top of the plates like a child rides on a raft in the water!*

Some plates are getting bigger at sites where new crustal material is being formed. For example, active rift volcanoes under the **Mid-Atlantic Ridge** spew magma through the ocean floor, which moves upward into cracks in the ridges and forces them apart, adding new crust. The Atlantic Ocean widens a little each year. Thus the plates holding the United States and Europe are spreading further apart.

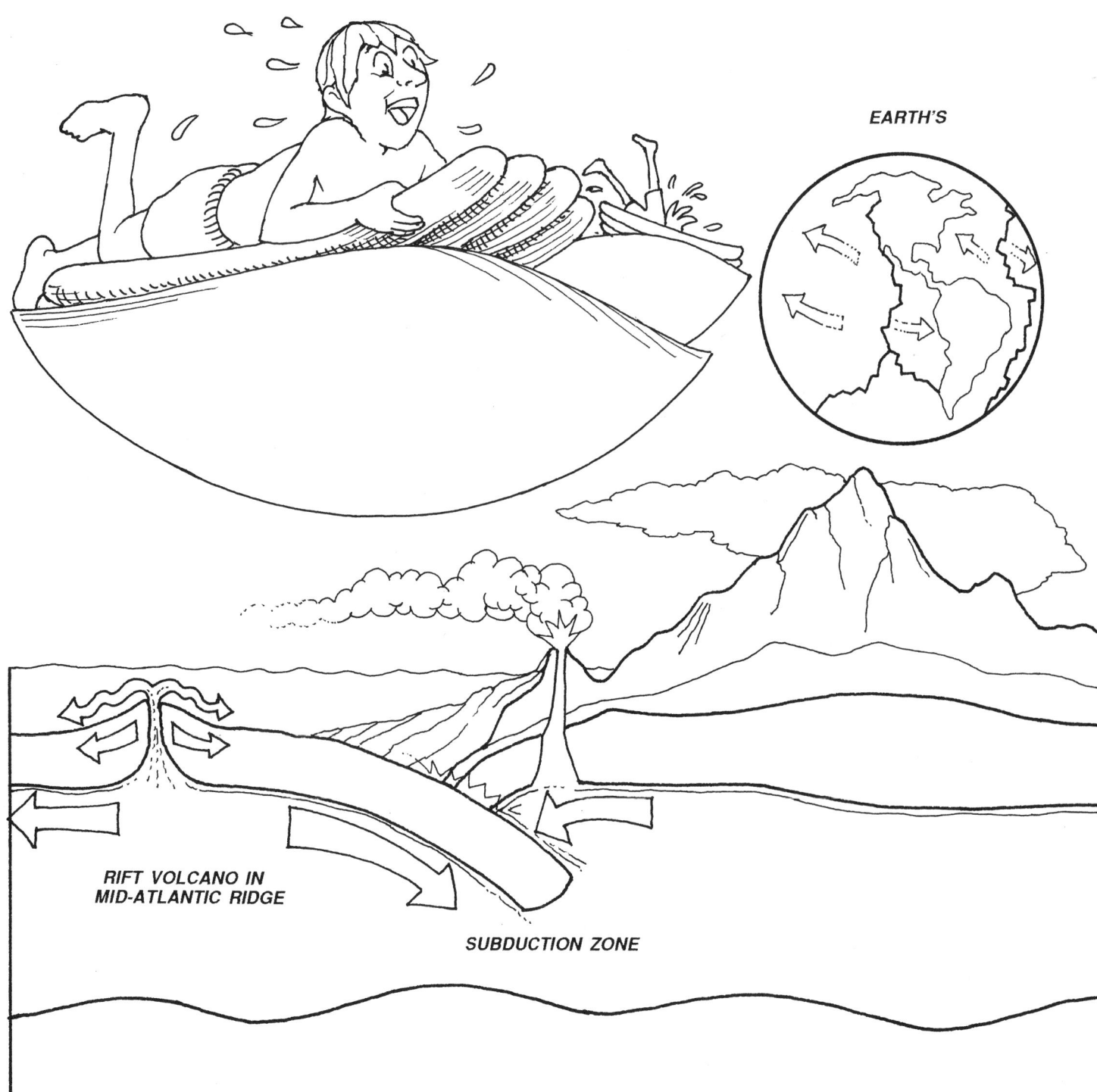

EARTH'S

RIFT VOLCANO IN MID-ATLANTIC RIDGE

SUBDUCTION ZONE

When the plates move together or converge, one may be forced under the other and down into the mantle. This is called a **subduction zone** and it is where ocean trenches are formed. It is very common for these areas to have **seismic** activity. Earthquakes occur when two plates rub or grind together.

Subduction volcanoes often develop at the **convergence site.** When one of the plates sinks, friction and heat from the mantle cause the plate to melt. The melted part may become magma and rises through deep faults or cracks to the surface to form volcanoes.

Hot spots are places in the ocean floor where hot magma breaks through weak spots in the crustal plate and forms volcanoes as the plate moves over this area. If underwater volcanoes continue to erupt and grow, the magma, which is called lava once it is outside the volcano, builds up thicker and deeper. Sometimes, the volcano will emerge above the ocean surface. When this happens, a volcanic island has formed. The islands in the Hawaiian archipelago and Society Islands began over hot spots.

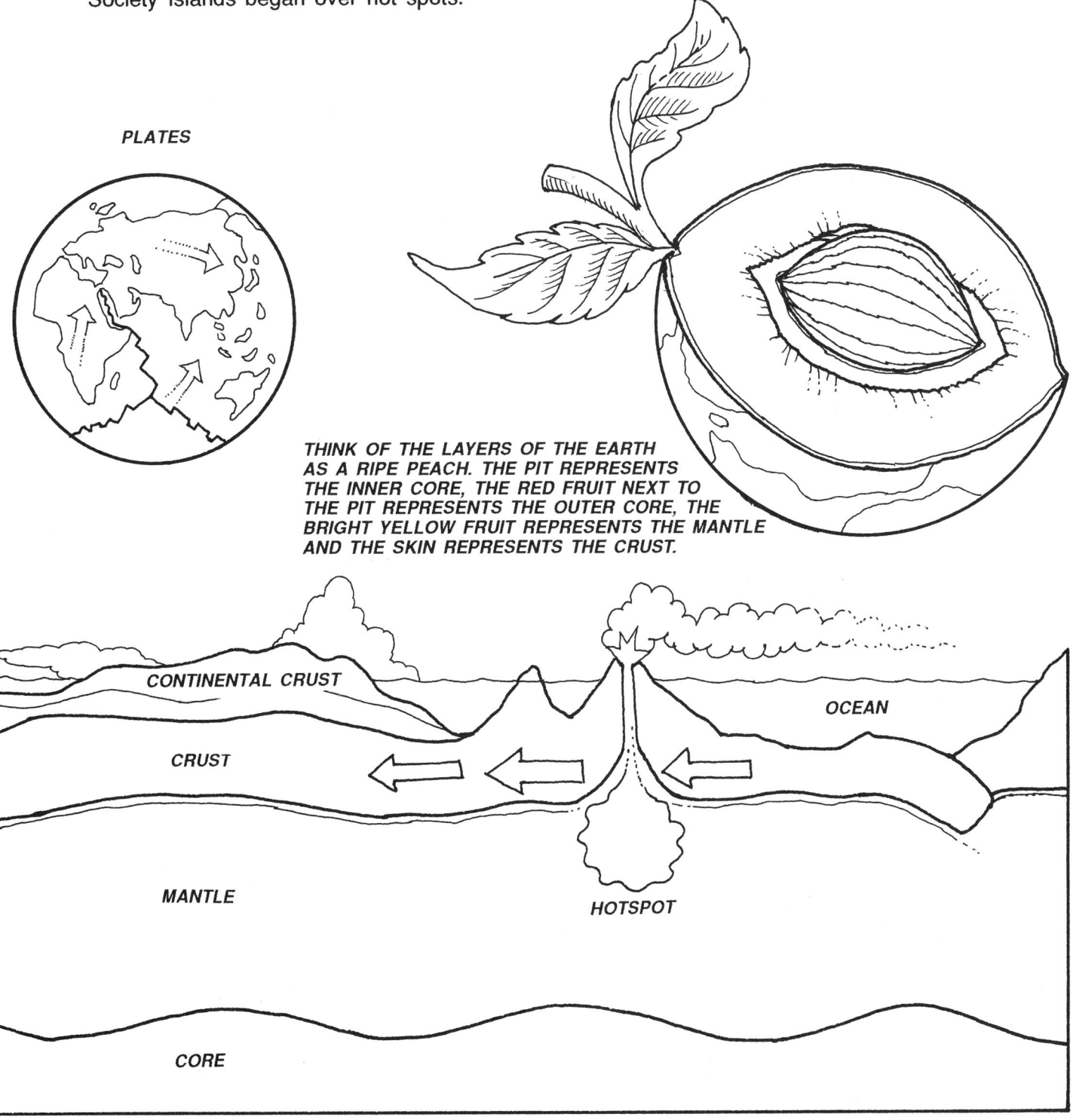

PLATES

THINK OF THE LAYERS OF THE EARTH AS A RIPE PEACH. THE PIT REPRESENTS THE INNER CORE, THE RED FRUIT NEXT TO THE PIT REPRESENTS THE OUTER CORE, THE BRIGHT YELLOW FRUIT REPRESENTS THE MANTLE AND THE SKIN REPRESENTS THE CRUST.

CONTINENTAL CRUST

OCEAN

CRUST

MANTLE

HOTSPOT

CORE

HYDROLOGIC CYCLE

Almost all the water on our planet has been here since the earth cooled. Small amounts of new water come from volcanic action, where hydrogen and oxygen combine to make water molecules in the state of steam. This means that the water you drink today could have been part of a dinosaur millions of years ago!

The hydrologic cycle of **evaporation, condensation,** and **precipitation** connects all the bodies of water on our earth.

In the beginning, the ocean was almost as salty as it is now. Salts and minerals are carried into the oceans from the land and rocks.

All the minerals in the earth's crust are found in the ocean—even gold and silver! Draw conclusions as to why this might be true.

How many types of evaporation can you find in the drawing?

How many types of precipitation can you find in the drawing? Can you think of any more types of precipitation?

Trace the path of a raindrop through the hydrologic cycle.

Predict how water that is evaporating from the Amazon River in South America may one day fall as rain on the African plain.

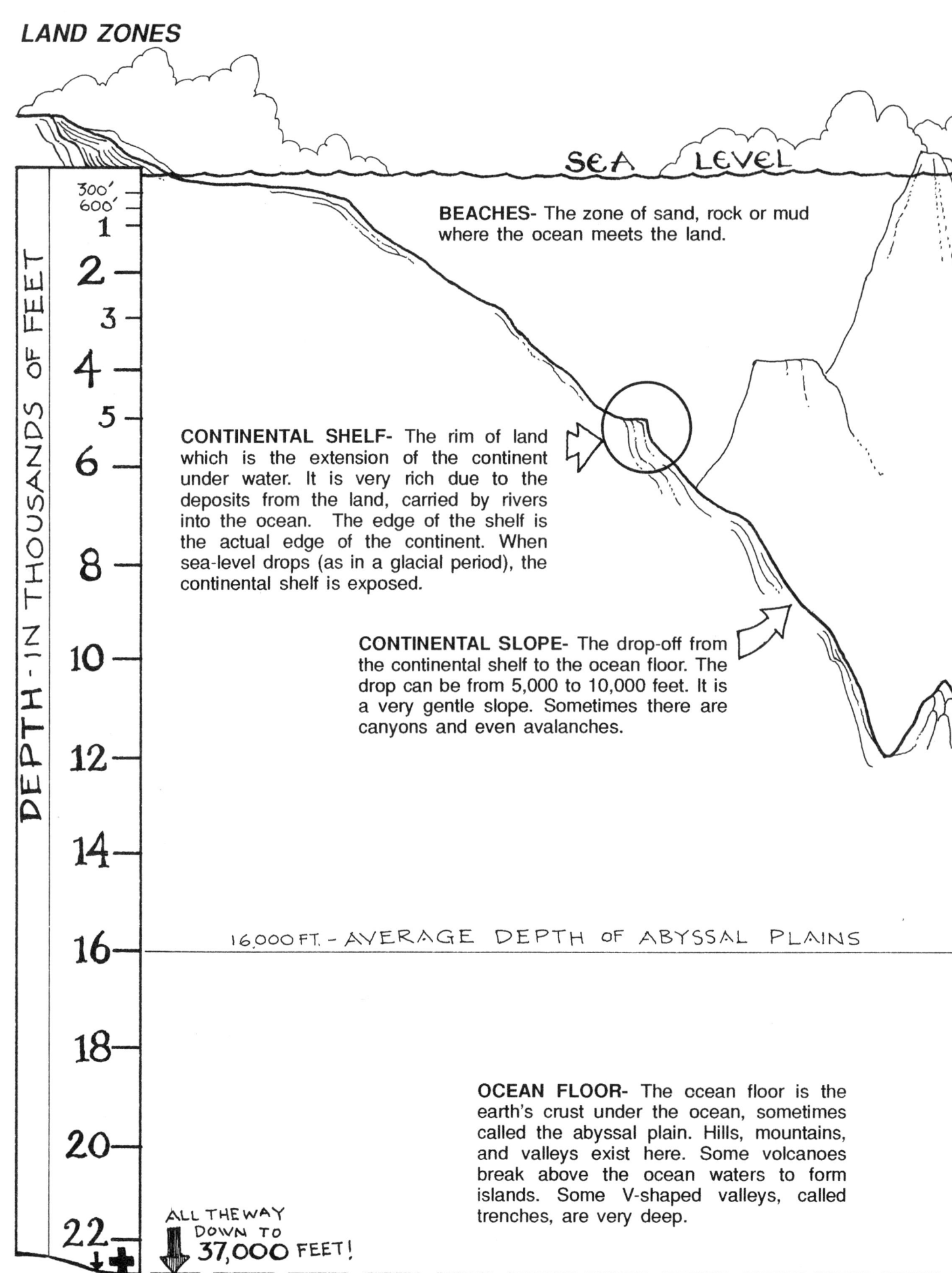

LIGHT ZONES

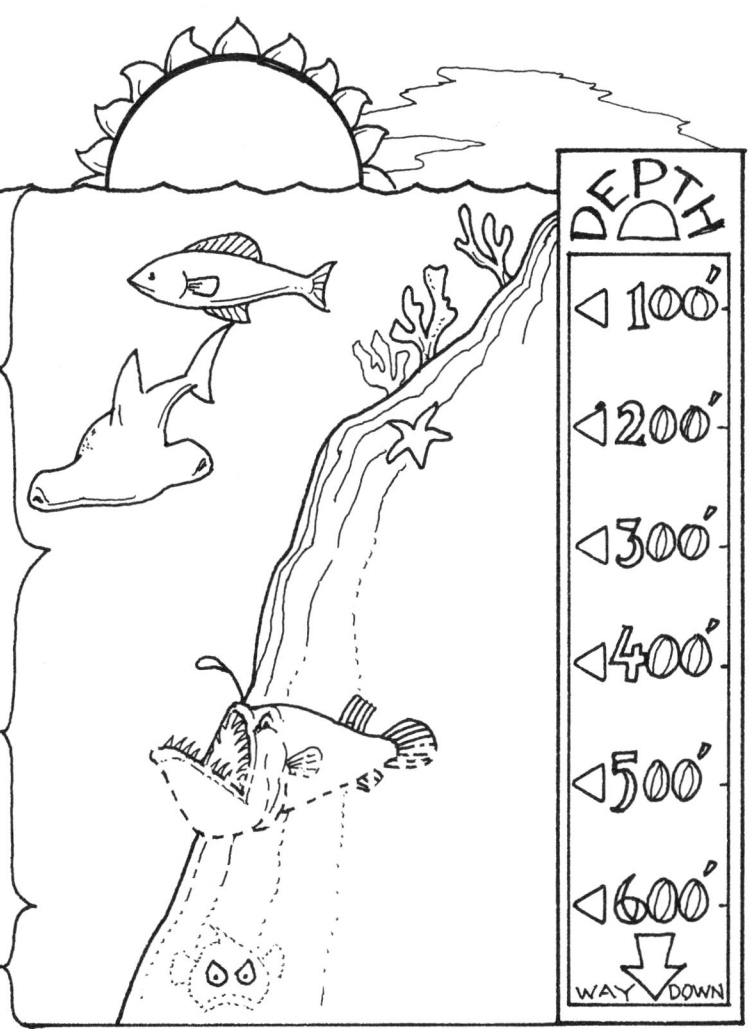

SURFACE (EUPHOTIC) ZONE- Water near the shore or in the ocean where enough light penetrates so that photosynthesis can occur. The depth of penetration depends on the clarity of the water. It can be a few feet in muddy waters or as much as 300 feet in deep ocean or near coral reefs. This is where seaweed and tiny one-celled plants can grow.

TWILIGHT (DISPHOTIC) ZONE -Water near the continental shelf and the top of the continental slope or open ocean to a depth of about 600 feet. Some light penetrates to this level, but very little. Many fish carry their own light and migrate up to feed.

DARK (APHOTIC) ZONE- Water at the bottom of the continental slope and on the ocean floor. There is no light here.

OCEAN RIDGES- Volcanic rift systems form long mountain ranges on the ocean floor. The longest mountain ridge in the world is under the ocean. It stretches nearly 40,000 miles along the Atlantic, Indian, Antarctic, and Pacific Oceans. The ridges are at the edge of the crustal plates.

THERMAL VENT- A crack in the ocean floor where ocean water seeps down to the hot rocks inside the earth, is warmed, and then resurfaces, is known as a thermal vent. The heated water is rich in hydrogen sulfide gas. Special bacteria are able to make food using heat energy and gas from the vent. This food sustains life near the vents which would not be able to live there otherwise.

CURRENTS

Imagine a river forty miles wide and two thousand feet deep, carrying water from the Gulf of Mexico and the west coast of Africa, north to Canada and then east to Europe. **The Gulf Stream** is such a river, flowing through the Atlantic Ocean. The Gulf Stream is one of many surface currents circulating in the earth's oceans. Because currents are a different temperature from the surrounding ocean waters, they affect the climate of the nearby land masses. The Gulf Stream affects the climate of the east coast of the United States, Norway and the British Isles.

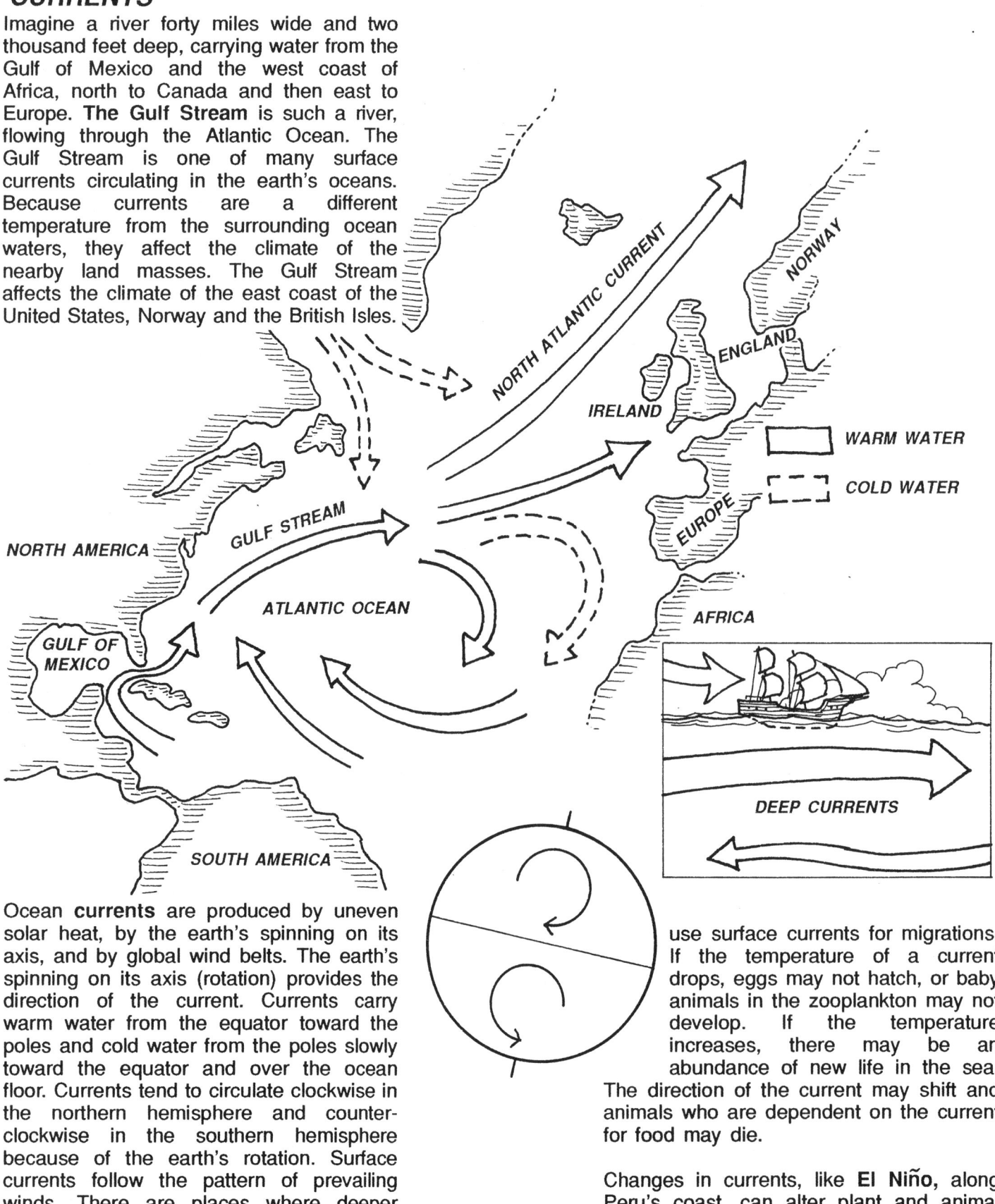

Ocean **currents** are produced by uneven solar heat, by the earth's spinning on its axis, and by global wind belts. The earth's spinning on its axis (rotation) provides the direction of the current. Currents carry warm water from the equator toward the poles and cold water from the poles slowly toward the equator and over the ocean floor. Currents tend to circulate clockwise in the northern hemisphere and counter-clockwise in the southern hemisphere because of the earth's rotation. Surface currents follow the pattern of prevailing winds. There are places where deeper currents actually flow beneath surface currents, heading in the opposite direction.

Currents carry oxygen, nutrients, plants, and animals. Life in the sea often depends on currents. Turtles, eels, and even whales use surface currents for migrations. If the temperature of a current drops, eggs may not hatch, or baby animals in the zooplankton may not develop. If the temperature increases, there may be an abundance of new life in the sea. The direction of the current may shift and animals who are dependent on the current for food may die.

Changes in currents, like **El Niño,** along Peru's coast, can alter plant and animal life. In this case, the rich, cold bottom waters are not brought up to the surface. There are fewer plants in the warmer, nutrient-poor surface waters where birds, fish, and sea-lions feed. Therefore, there is less food available.

TIDES

The periodic rise and fall of the earth's water, the **tides**, is caused by the strong gravitational pull of the moon and the sun. Even though the sun is much larger, the moon has a stronger pull on the tides because it is closer to the earth. When the moon is directly over the ocean, the water is pulled towards it. The water on the other side of the planet is also pulled outward, like a bulge, because of centrifugal force caused by the rotation of the earth.

There are areas on the earth that have **semidiurnal** tides, which means that they have two high and two low tides a day. **Diurnal** tides are when there is only one high and low tide per day. Some areas have **mixed** tides.

The lunar day is twenty-four hours and fifty minutes long. Tides will therefore be fifty minutes later each day than the day before. It is very easy to predict and chart the tidal movements.

All water is subject to daily tidal forces. We can see it best where the continents meet the ocean waters. The water rises and falls on the shore. This is the intertidal zone. When the tide is rising (**flood tide**), the ocean water is bringing nutrients, oxygen, and eggs or larva to the estuaries, marshes, and intertidal zone. The falling tide (**ebb tide**) moves sediment, decaying plant materials, and nutrients to the sea. **Tidal currents** are formed by patterns of ebb and flood tides around the edges of sounds, bays, and inlets.

Twice a month tides are either higher (Spring tide) or lower (Neap tide) than average. **Spring tides** rise higher and fall lower than other tides. They occur when the moon is full or new, and the earth, sun, and moon are in a straight line. The gravitational pull is stronger because the sun and moon are working together in the tidal pull.

Neap tides have the least amount of change in **tidal range** (the vertical distance between high and low tide). They occur when the moon is in quarter stages, and the sun, moon, and earth are at right angles. The moon's gravitational pull is weakened by the sun's gravitational pull.

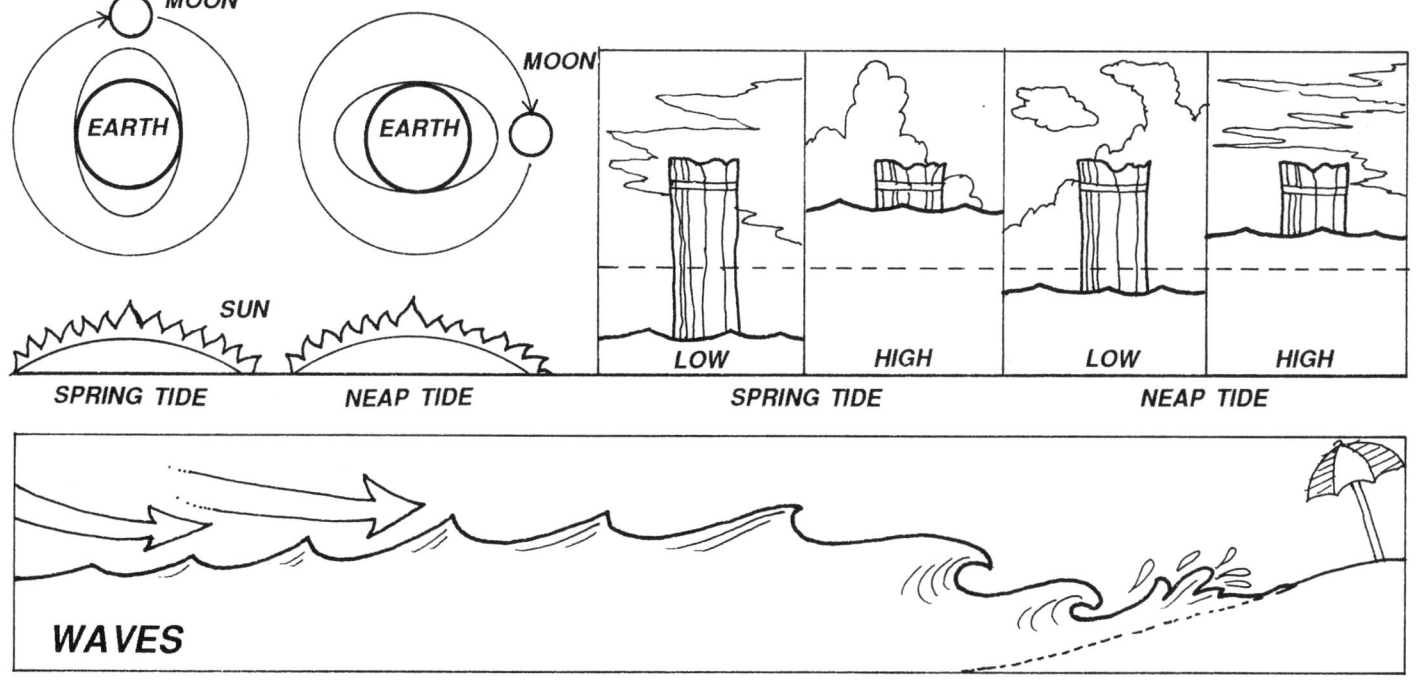

WAVES

Most waves are caused by the wind as it blows across the water. Wave size is affected by the strength of the wind, the length of time it blows, and the distance across the water that the wind blows without being held back by land. Although water in the ocean appears to be moving forward when we see waves, it really is not. Wave energy moves *through* the water. The water just rotates, almost in place. **Breakers** occur when the cycle of rotation is interrupted by the land. Not all events called tides are caused by the moon. Tidal waves, called **Tsunamis**, are huge waves that are actually caused by undersea earthquakes. Storm surges are also waves of higher ocean waters brought to the shore by hurricanes.

SPECIES: BLUE CRAB

Unlike people, some animals wear their skeleton on the outside! A **crustacean** has a hard shell that protects its soft body like a suit of armor. Crustaceans also have jointed legs, so they are classified in the phylum **Arthropoda**. Insects and spiders are also arthropods.

A common Atlantic coast crustacean is the **blue crab**. These crabs live in **estuaries** like the Chesapeake Bay. They like **brackish water**, which is a mixture of salt water and river water. Only the females migrate out to the ocean where they lay their eggs.

Blue crabs have five pair of jointed legs. The front pair are claws for feeding and defense. The next three pairs of legs are used for walking. These crabs walk sideways and can move pretty fast! The back pair of legs are modified into paddles for swimming. Blue crabs are terrific swimmers. If a crab's leg is hurt, it can grow a new one in the next molt. This process is called **regeneration**.

Blue crabs have excellent vision. The eyes are on **stalks**, so they can see in almost any direction. Between their eyes, there are **antennae** for touching and tasting. Crabs eat almost anything, whether plant or animal, including fish, snails, clams, shrimp, mole crabs, and oysters. Sometimes they are even cannibals, eating other crabs!

A crustacean's **carapace** (shell) doesn't grow or stretch. So for a crab to get bigger, it has to shed its shell. This is called **molting**. Crabbers have their own words to describe molting. They say that crabs who are ready to "bust" are "peelers." Their old shell splits, and the crab backs out of the shell—legs, body and even eyestalks! The new shell is soft. It takes a few hours to a day to harden. While it is soft, people like to catch and eat them, shell and all! Male crabs molt throughout their lives, whereas females only molt until they are mature and ready to reproduce.

15

SCALLOPS

Mollusks are animals with no bones. Since they have no backbone or skeleton, many have **shells** to protect their bodies and attach muscles. Some of them even start building their shells inside the egg, before they hatch. If you have been to the beach, you might have guessed from all the shells on the shore that mollusks are the largest group of water animals. There are 100,000 kinds of living mollusks. New species are found frequently.

The mollusk's soft body is covered with a thin layer of skin called the **mantle**. On clams and scallops, the mantle shows at the edge of the shell, like a **fringe.** Shell material is secreted by the mantle and then hardens. As the mollusk grows, it adds material to its shell, and the shell grows too. Shells are made of **calcium carbonate**, like your bones. Mollusks get this material from the water.

CHECKLIST
PHYLUM: Mollusca
CLASS: Bivalvia

SPECIES: SCALLOP

What sea animal has "ears" and **siphons**, rows of blue eyes, and seems to travel by jet propulsion? A scallop!

Scallops are **bivalve** mollusks. They have two shells which are hinged together. Scallops get their name from their wavy-edged shell. Some scallops have wing-like projections called "ears" near the hinge. The inside of the living shell is lined with tissue called the mantle. The edge of the mantle is folded and fringed with tentacles and rows of blue eyes. The scallop can sense light and dark through its eyes. This is enough so when an enemy (like a sea star) approaches, it can move away quickly.

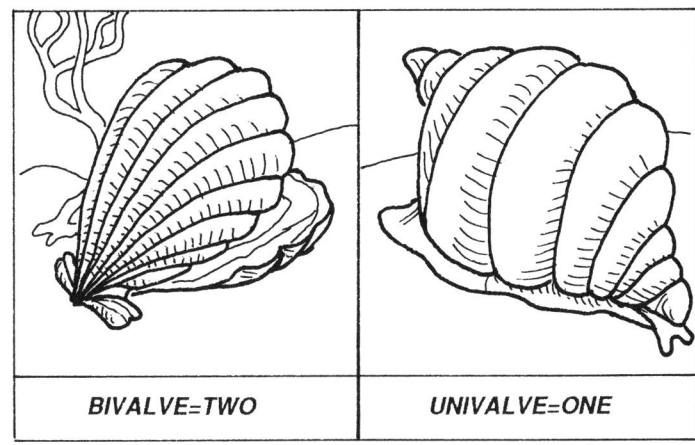

BIVALVE=TWO UNIVALVE=ONE

A scallop moves by forcing water through siphons. It quickly opens and closes its shells. It can jet a yard or more with a single "squirt."

Scallops live in waters throughout the world. Some live in waters up to four and one-half miles deep. Their shells are usually open as they rest and feed on the ocean floor. Seawater carrying food is filtered through the **gills**. The scallop has two siphons for feeding. One draws in seawater and the other ejects it out after the tiny plankton have been removed.

A scallop's shell grows with the soft body. The two shells are not the same shape and color. The top shell has more curve, while the bottom shell is flatter. Colors range from red, purple, yellow, and brown to white. The shells are from one to eight inches across.

The muscle which opens and closes the scallop shell is the part commonly eaten by people.

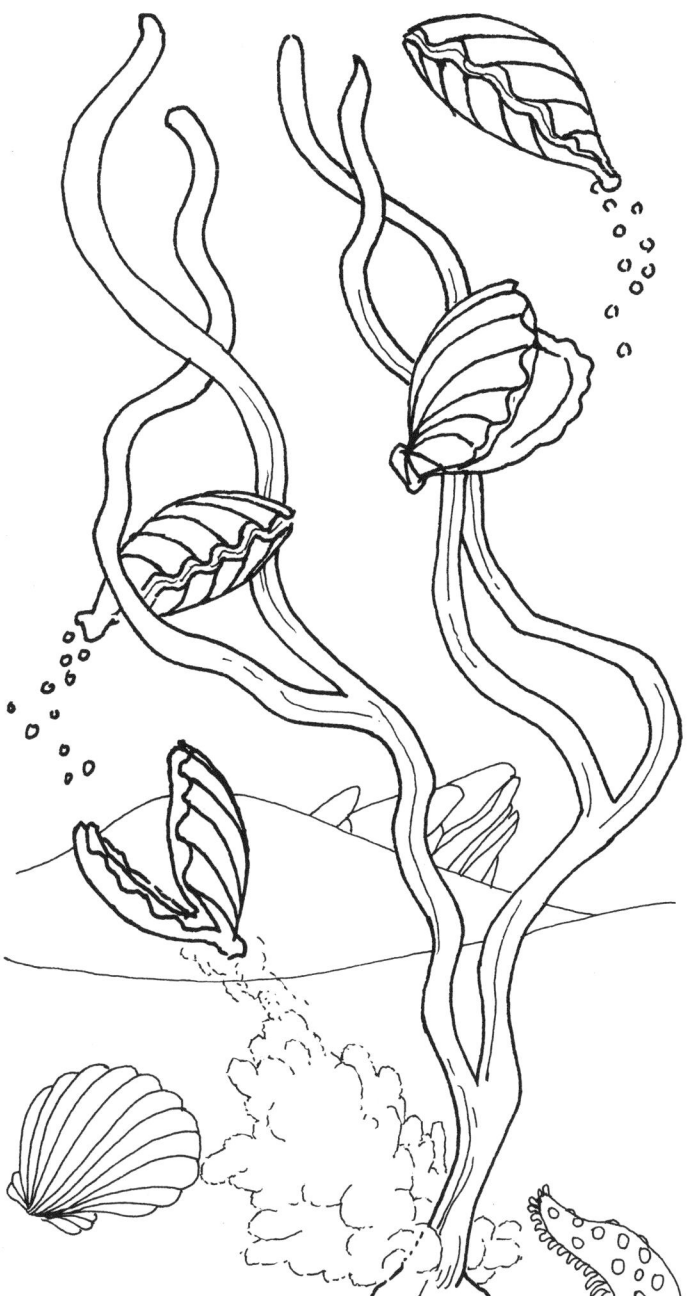

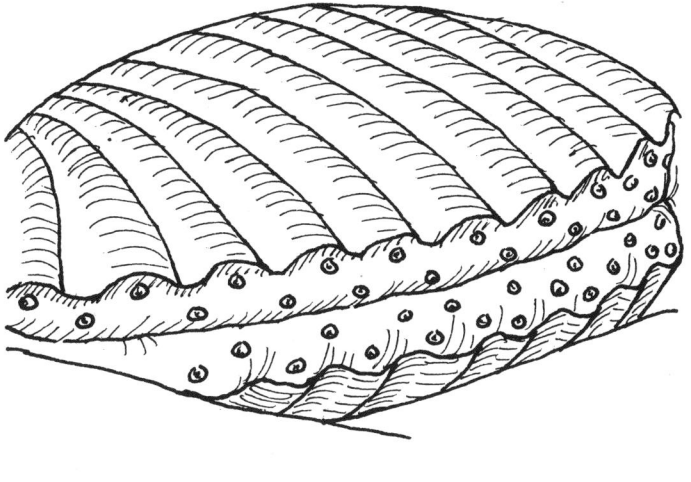

17

SPECIES: SEA STAR

Echinoderms are spiny-skinned sea animals. Sea stars, sand dollars, and sea urchins are all types of echinoderms. All these animals have **radial symmetry**. Their body parts are arranged around the center like spokes around the hub of a wheel. Most echinoderms have **tubefeet**, which they use for moving and feeding.

The body of the common starfish (another name for sea stars) has a **central disk** with five arms radiating from it. Other varieties of sea stars have up to fifty arms. There is a groove down the center of each arm, which is filled with rows of tubes called tubefeet. Sea stars can have up to 40,000 feet! **Suction discs** at the end of each tubefoot enable the sea star to move or to feed. These discs can grip and slowly pry open the sea star's prey. The round dot on top of the sea star is the **madreporite** or sieve plate. It pumps water and sends it through the tubes in the sea star's arms. The force of the water helps the sea star to move across the ocean floor at the rate of about six inches a minute. With so many feet, you would think it could move faster!

The sea star has no brain and no eyes, but it does have eyespots at the end of each arm. These spots are sensitive to light and dark, but they do not "see" shapes. The sea star's mouth is on the underside of its body in the center.

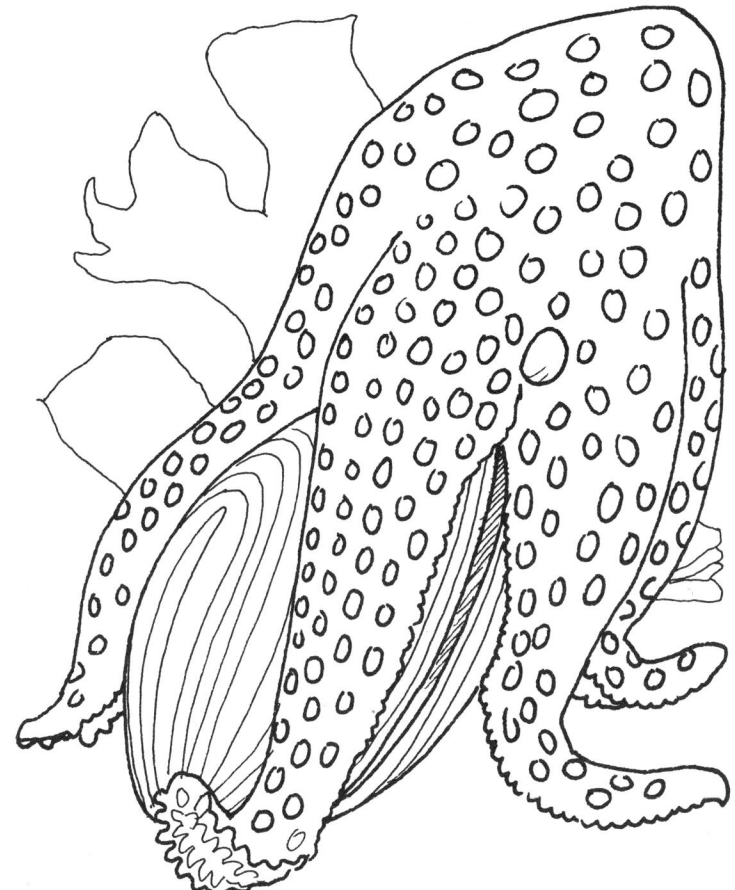

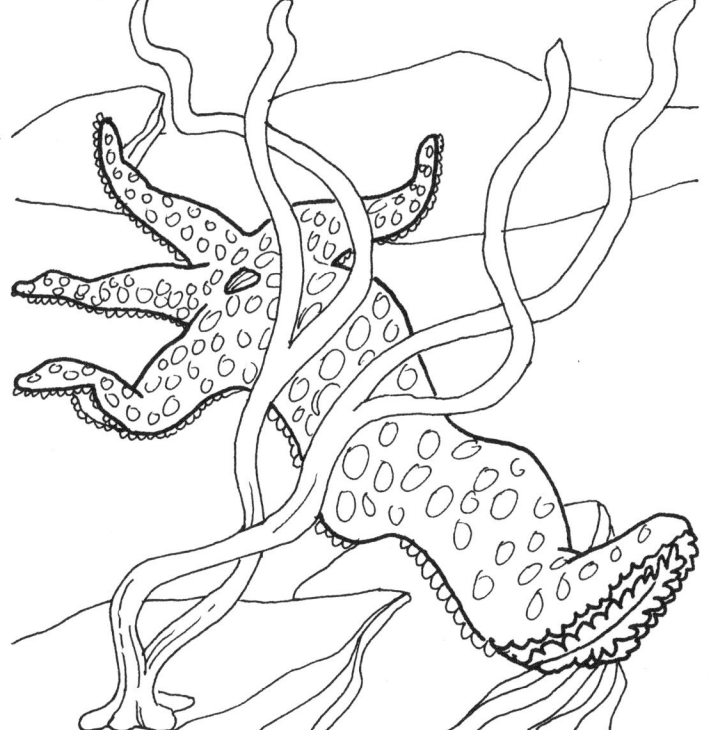

Sea stars are hunters and scavengers, feeding mainly on scallops, clams, or oysters. The sea star has a most astonishing manner of eating! When it has used **suction** to pry the two shells apart a little, it pushes its stomach out of its mouth and in between the shells. The stomach secretes juices called **enzymes**, which digest the prey. When it is through, the sea star pulls its stomach back in.

A sea star can **regenerate** a new arm if one breaks off. Fishermen, considering sea stars pests, used to tear them in half and throw them back in the water every time they found one. Little did they know, they were making double the trouble, because two new starfish grew out of the two halves!

A **comet** is a new sea star that develops from the dropped-off arm of another sea star. Just as there are stars in the sea as well as the sky, there are also comets in the sea and sky.

WHERE CAN WE LOOK TO FIND STARS? THERE ARE MANY IN THE SEA! JUST AS THERE ARE STARS IN THE SKY, MANY TYPES OF SEA STARS LIVE IN THE DEEP OCEANS AND IN SHALLOW WATERS ALONG THE SHORES TODAY.

WHO EATS WHOM ?

Food chains in the ocean interlock and overlap to form **food webs.** Most animals rely on more than one source of food and most foods are eaten by more than one kind of animal.

Food relationships can be represented by a trophic pyramid. The trophic pyramid shows how each animal receives nourishment and each one in turn becomes nourishment to other animals.

Working from the base level of the trophic pyramid, it takes about 10,000 pounds of diatoms found in the phytoplankton to produce one pound of killer whale at the top of the pyramid. Baleen whales utilize the lower level of the food chain and eat plankton directly. By eating 10,000 pounds of diatoms, a baleen whale can yield 100 pounds of growth. This is a very efficient transfer of energy to a large animal.

Plants harvest energy from the sun through photosynthesis. Plants are therefore the first link in the food chain. Animals ultimately depend on plants for their energy. **Phytoplankton** are tiny one-celled plants that are the basic food supply of the ocean. Most animals feed on them either directly or indirectly. They are the producers at the base of the food chain in the ocean and provide as much as 80% of the world's organic material and oxygen.

Animals are consumers and form all upper links in the food chain. **Zooplankton** is made up of tiny animals which feed on phytoplankton. Many zooplankters are young larvae of fish and invertebrates like crabs and shrimp. Small fish eat zooplankton. Larger fish eat small fish.

The remains of dead plants (**detritus**) and animals are eaten by scavengers.

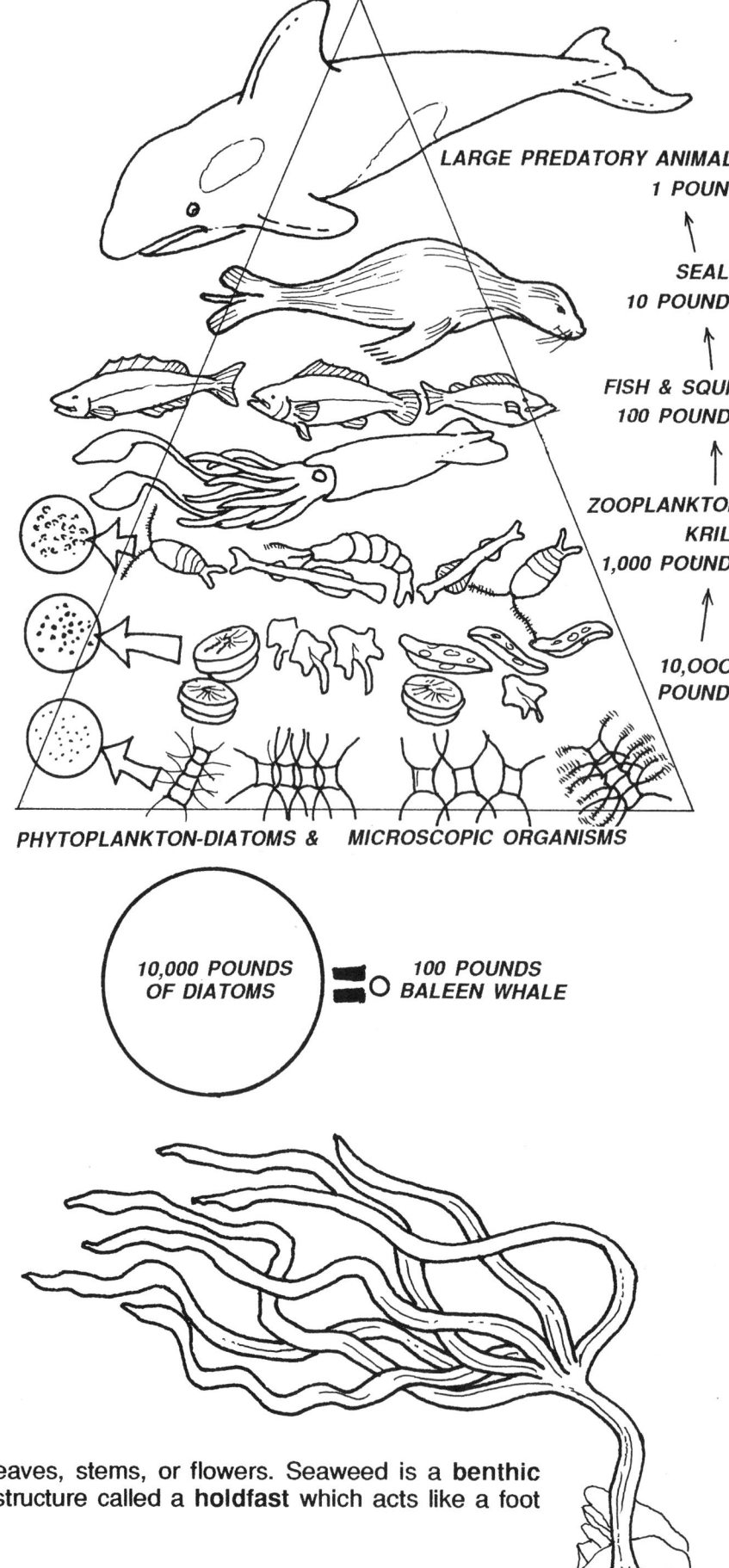

SEAWEED

Seaweed is **algae**. It does not have roots, leaves, stems, or flowers. Seaweed is a **benthic** plant that keeps itself attached by a special structure called a **holdfast** which acts like a foot to keep it in place.

Seaweed is grouped by color and the chemical make-up of its pigment into blue-green algae, green algae, red algae, and brown algae. It is important not only because it is a food producer but because it releases large amounts of oxygen during photosynthesis.

AND WHERE?

PLANKTON- Both animal and plant plankton **float** in the water. They are unable to move on their own and therefore are at the will of the ocean's tides, currents, and waves to move them. Phytoplankton need to be near the surface so that the sunlight is available for photosynthesis. Zooplankton feed on phytoplankton, so they are mainly near the surface.

When plankton species bloom in great numbers, they seem to change the color of the ocean water. "Red Tide" is an example of a quickly reproducing plankton that stains the water reddish. These plankton die and release toxins into the water that can kill fish.

NEKTON- Any animal that can **swim** freely of currents, tides, or waves is part of the nekton. Fish, turtles, reptiles, and marine mammals are part of this group. The only invertebrate that swims strongly enough to be classified as nekton is the squid.

BENTHOS- Any organism, plant or animal, that lives on the ocean bottom is part of the **benthos.** Seaweed and sea grasses, sponges, anemones, snails, crabs, and corals are examples of benthic life.

FUN AND GAMES

Crabbers call a male blue crab a "jimmy," an immature female a "sally," and a mature female a "sook." Predict which are larger, jimmys, sallys, or sooks. Give reasons for your answer.

How is a crab like a medieval knight?

Why is a grouchy person called a crab?

What if your skeleton was on the outside?

CRABBY CROSSWORDS

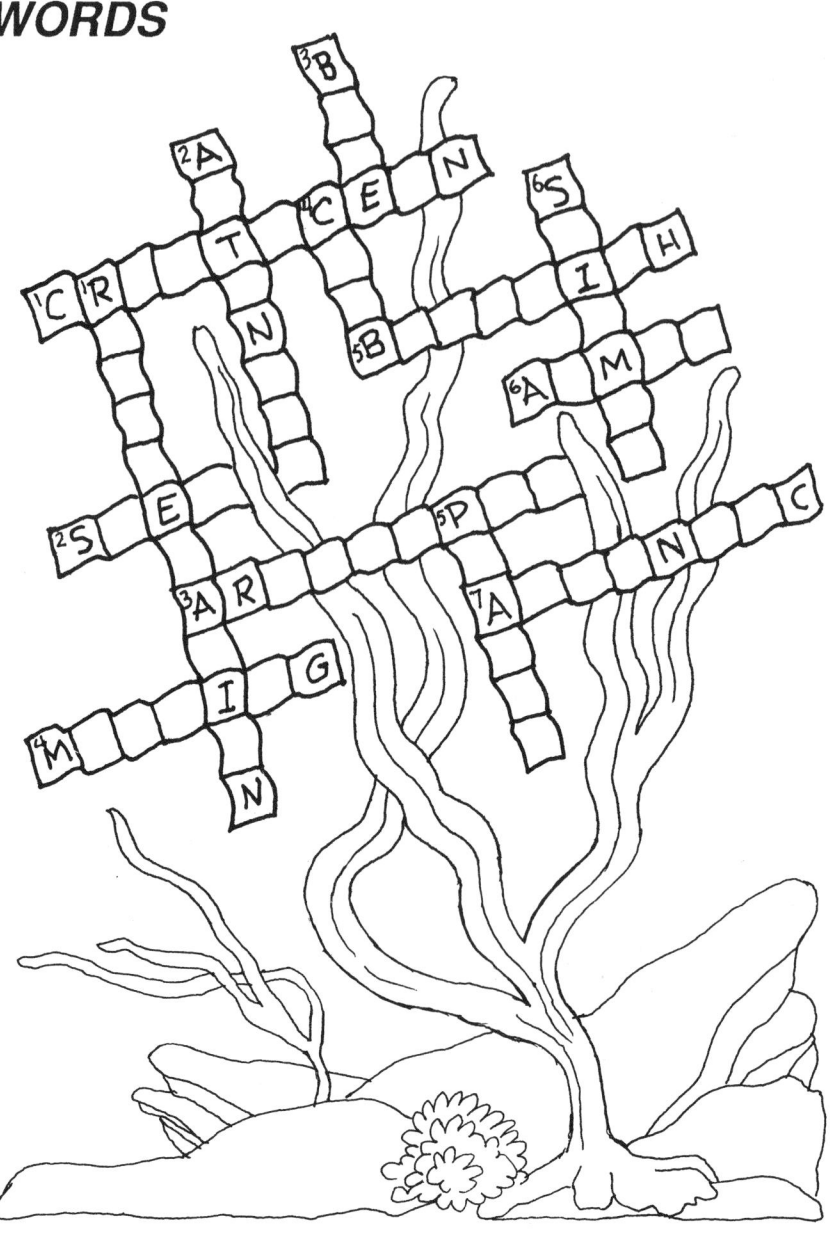

CLUES ACROSS

1. AN ANIMAL THAT HAS ITS SKELETON ON THE OUTSIDE
2. TO THROW OFF
3. THE FAMILY OF ANIMALS THAT HAVE JOINTED LEGS
4. THE PROCESS OF SHEDDING A SHELL
5. -------- WATER IS A MIXTURE OF SALT WATER AND FRESH WATER
6. WORN ON THE OUTSIDE FOR PROTECTION
7. THE OCEAN THAT DIVIDES EUROPE AND AFRICA FROM NORTH AND SOUTH AMERICA

CLUES DOWN

1. THE PROCESS OF GROWING ALL NEW PARTS
2. FEELERS THAT HELP ANIMALS TO FIND THEIR WAY AND TO FIND FOOD
3. A COLOR OF THE CRAB FOUND IN THE NORTHERN ATLANTIC
4. A CRUSTACEAN, ALSO A CROSS PERSON
5. SEAWEED, GRASS, FLOWERS ARE OFTEN CALLED BY THIS GENERAL TERM
6. A WORD FOR A PERSON OR OTHER ANIMAL WHO PROPELS HIMSELF THROUGH WATER

CRAB MOSAIC

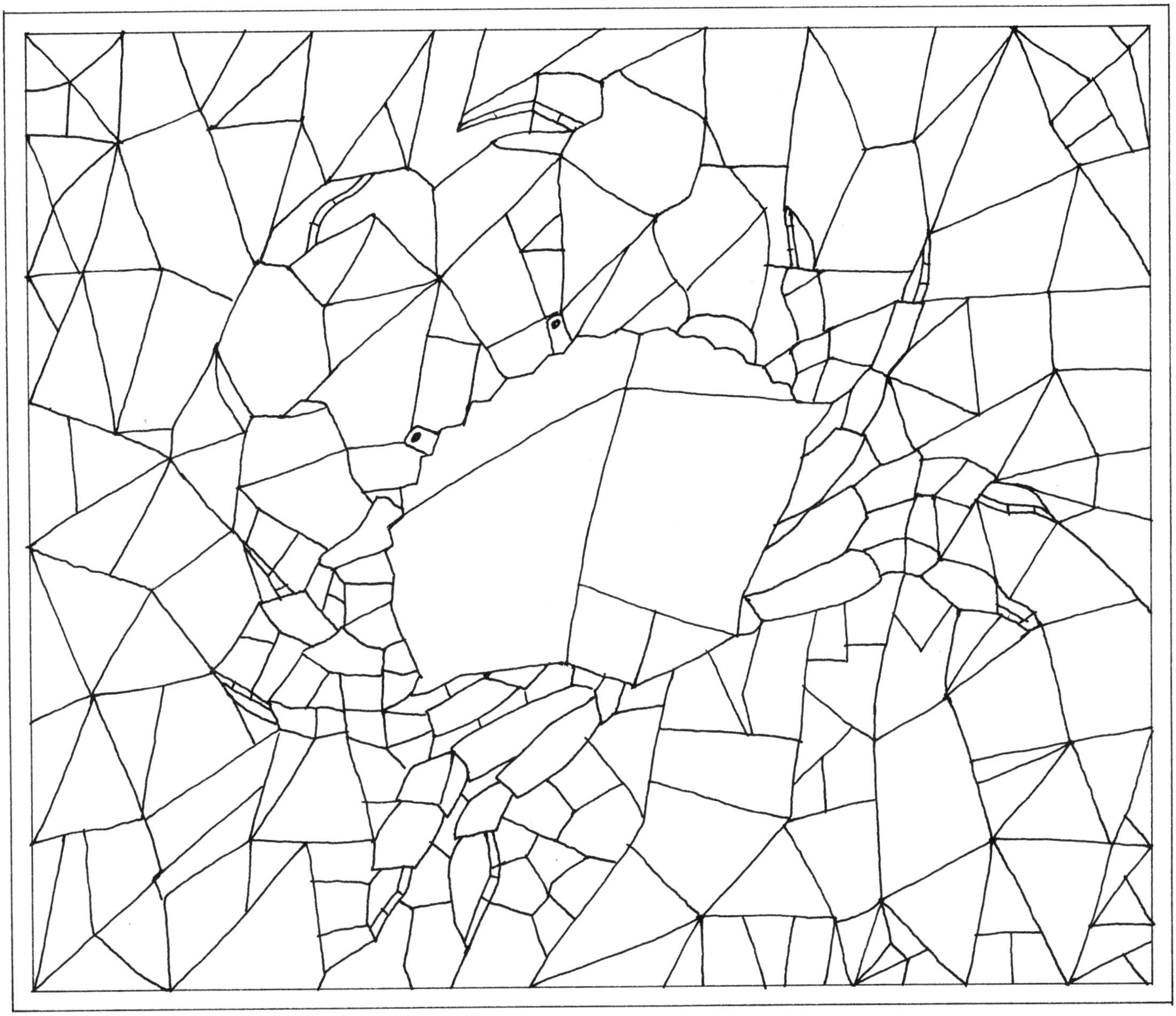

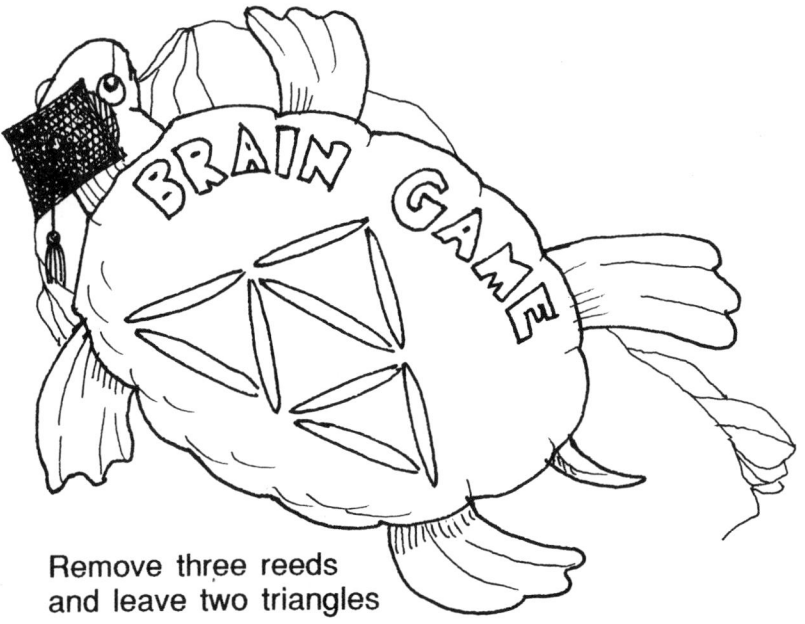

Remove three reeds
and leave two triangles

Create a myth about why the crab walks sideways.

●●●●●●●●●●●●●●

Tell a story about a crab who was afraid to molt.

FUN AND GAMES

POINTS TO PONDER

How did we get the terms clam up, happy as a clam, and clammy?

Can you think of other ways expressions in our language have their roots in animal behavior?

Predict what might happen if there were not enough calcium carbonate available for the clams to build their shells. How might this affect life in the ocean? On earth?

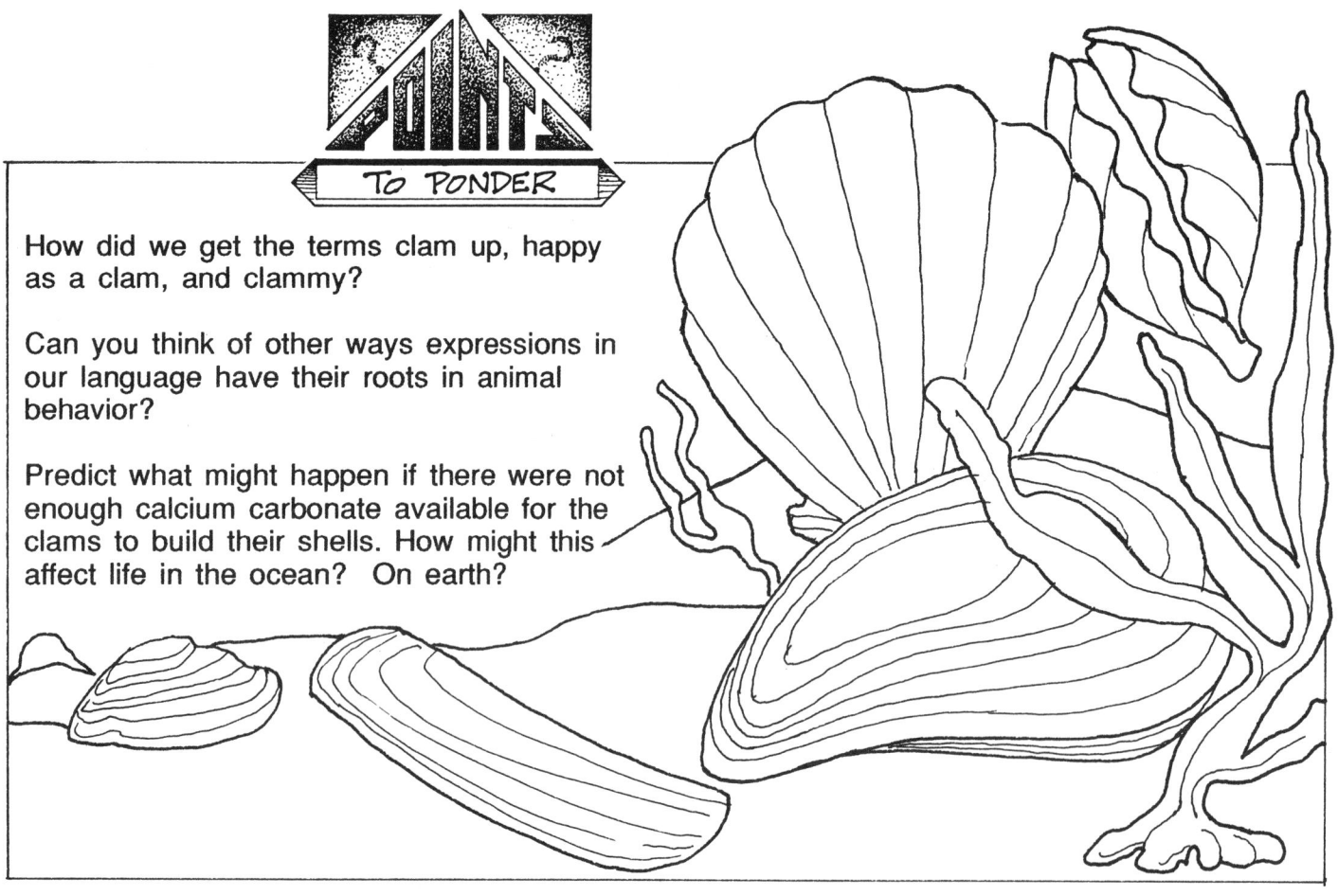

SCALLOP JUMBLE

DIRECTIONS: UNSCRAMBLE THE WORDS ASSOCIATED WITH SCALLOPS. THEN USE THE CIRCLED LETTERS TO UNSCRAMBLE THE MISSING WORD IN THE SENTENCE.

TANMEL _ _ ○ _ _ _

UILCACM RATAEOBCN _ _ _ _ _ _ _ _ _ _ _ ○ _ _ _ _

LIEVBAV _ ○ _ _ _ _ _

SLESHL _ ○ _ _ _ _

EJT SORPIPOULN _ _ _ ○ _ _ _ _ _ ○ _ _ _

CATELSENT _ _ _ _ _ _ ○ _ _

THE SCALLOP HAS TWO _____ TO HELP IT GET ITS FOOD FROM THE WATER.

CONNECT THE DOTS

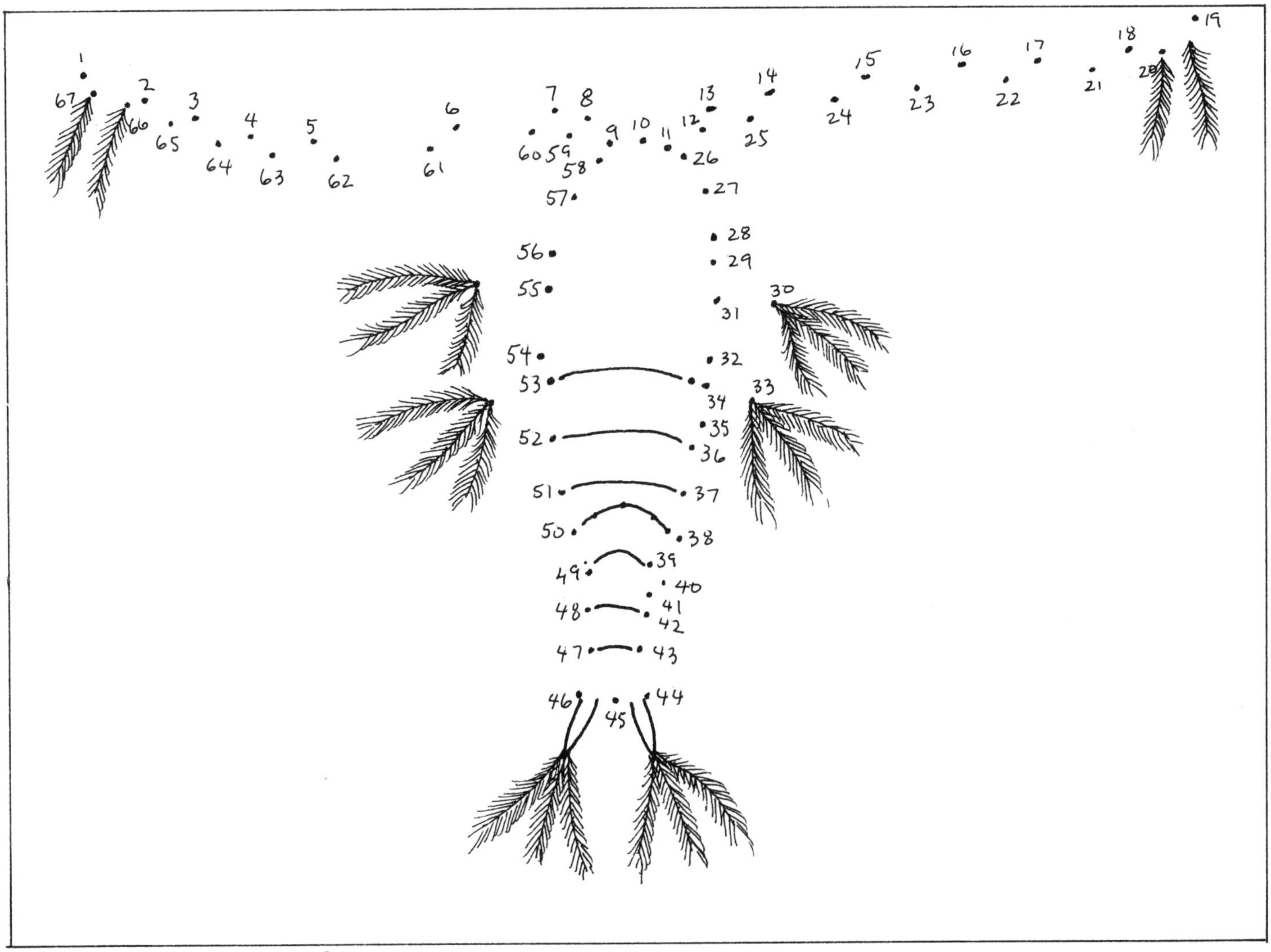

Add to this story: The little scallops in the bed off the coast of Peru listened with alarm to the whale's warning "El Niño! El Niño!"

●●●●●●●●●●●●●

Develop a myth: One day in the deep, deep sea King Neptune was strolling through his kingdom when he came across a scallop crying from its many blue eyes. Neptune stopped and asked_____?

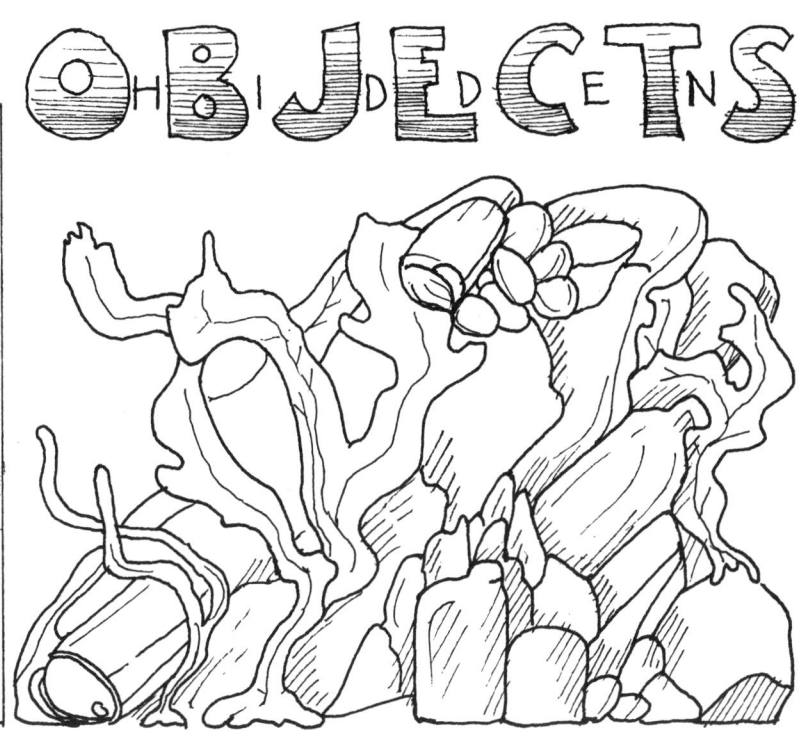

27

FUN AND GAMES

POINTS TO PONDER

Notice the class name for the sea star (asteroidea). Does that remind you of any other "heavenly" term?

Think of many, varied types of stars: Example- starry-eyed, star light.

How do you think man could benefit from a scientific study of the sea star's ability to regenerate parts?

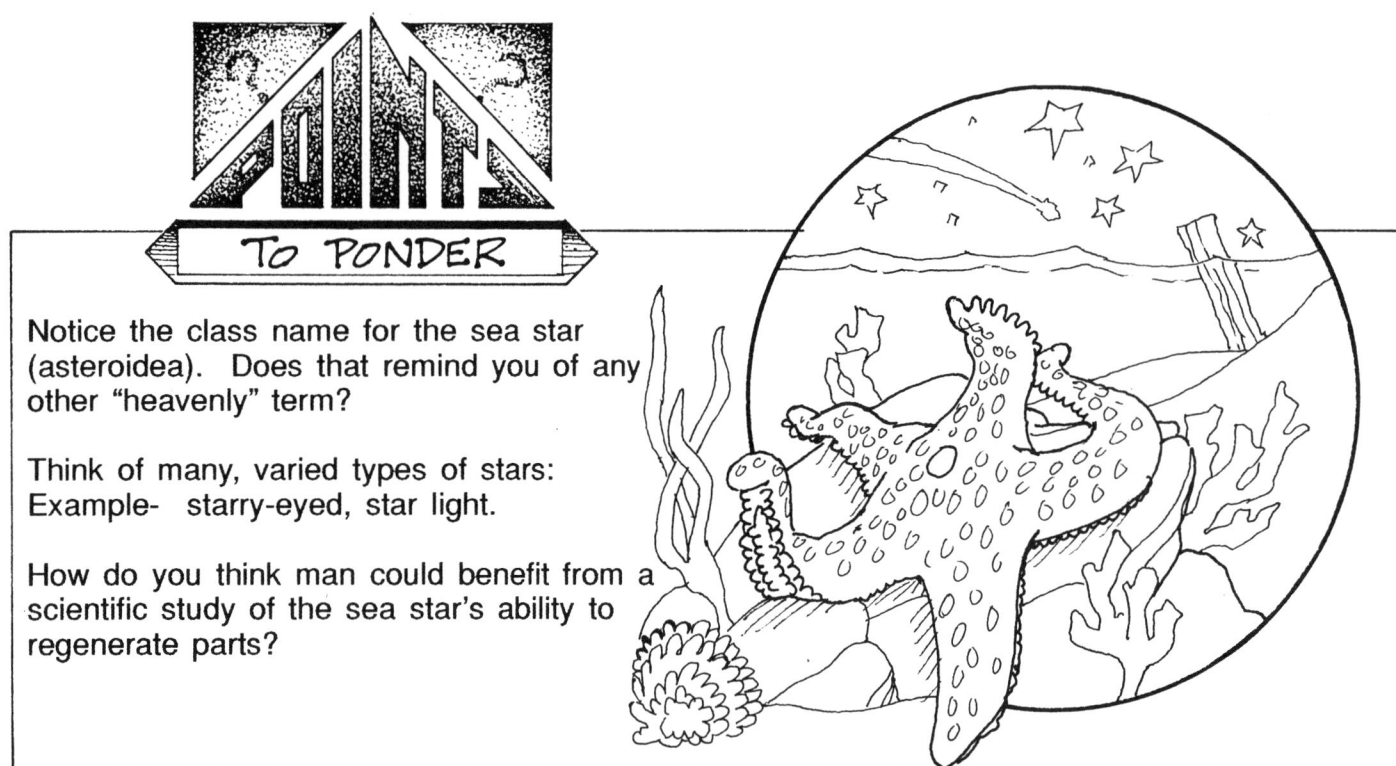

SEA STAR WORD FUN

DIRECTIONS: FIND AND SHADE THE LISTED WORDS. THE LETTERS THAT ARE NOT SHADED REVEAL A MESSAGE FOR YOU!

ECHINODERM
SPINY SKINNED
RADIAL SYMMETRY
PUMPS
TUBEFEET
GROOVE
SUCTION
MADREPORITE
EYESPOTS
HUNTERS
ENZYMES
REGENERATE
COMET
PESTS
EAT
PRY
ARMS

```
Y O U R S U C T I O N
C A N A P F M U I N D
C R S T D I A A B G R S
R E C H I N O D E R M A
E G O U A Y N R F O D C
G E M N L S O E E O E M
E N E T S K E P E V Y T
N E T E Y I S O T E E I
E R N R M N T R H E S S
R A K S M N Y I A N P P
A T D I E E N T T H O U
T E A T T D E E S E T M
E A ! P R Y P E S T S P
  E N Z Y M E S A R M S
```

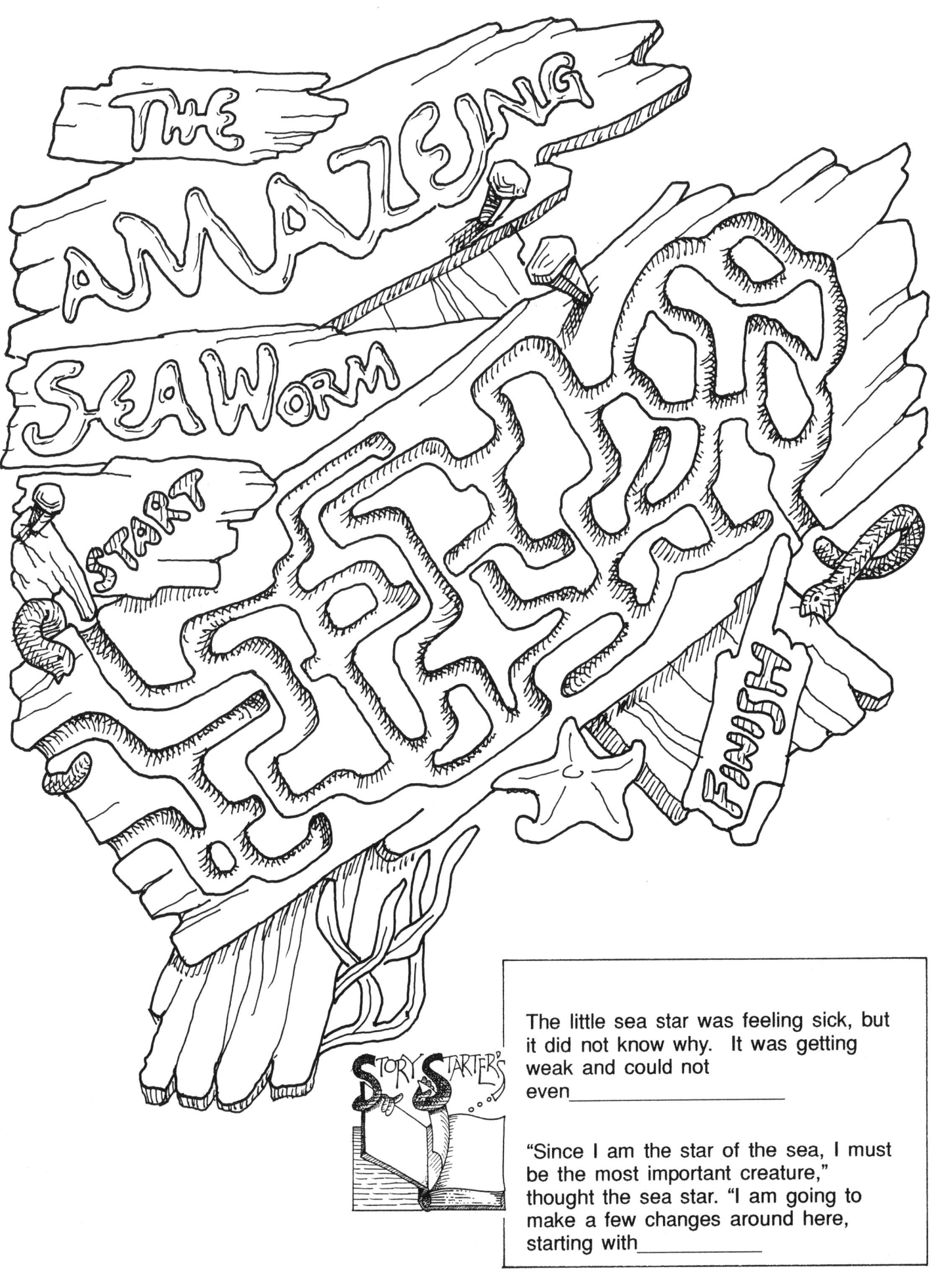

The little sea star was feeling sick, but it did not know why. It was getting weak and could not even_____

"Since I am the star of the sea, I must be the most important creature," thought the sea star. "I am going to make a few changes around here, starting with_____

SCIENCE EXPERIMENTS

PLATE TECTONICS, HOW DID THE ATLANTIC OCEAN GET THERE?

PURPOSE
To simulate the mid-Atlantic Ridge and to discover how ocean basins spread.

MATERIALS
A large sheet of paper, a marker or crayon, a table with a crack or two stacks of books

PROCEDURE
Fold the paper in half. Insert it between the two books or into the crack in the table. Crease part of the left side of the paper and fold it over the table. Label this part "North America". Crease part of the right side and fold it over on the table. Label it "Africa". This simulates the single, joined continent before it breaks up.

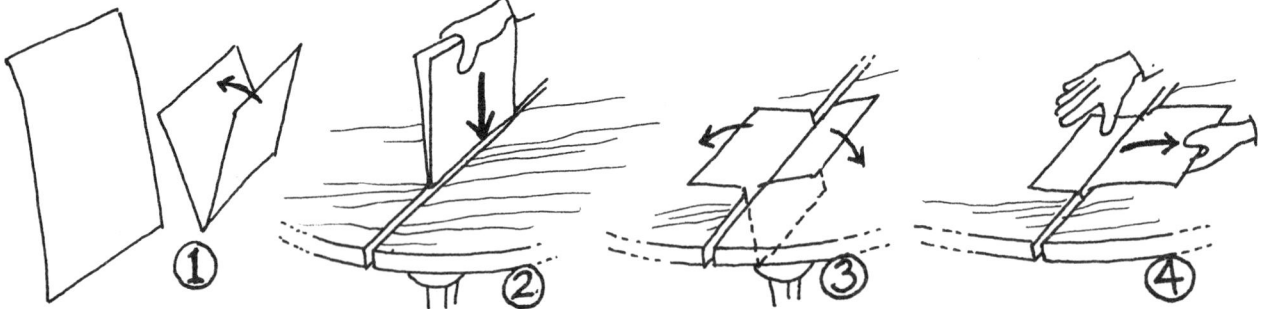

Slowly pull each half from the center. This represents the rift or split of the supercontinent (Pangae). As the rift becomes wider, color it blue. This represents the ocean basin.

Pull the rift out farther and color the new part blue. The Atlantic Ocean is continuing to widen. The place where the rift begins is in the mid-Atlantic Ridge--a chain of volcanic mountains extending north of Iceland and south of Africa.

●●●

BATHTUB, WASHTUB, OR THE KITCHEN SINK

There are many scientific experiments that you can do with just a little water and a few items from around the house. Next time you are in the bathtub, try to create waves by blowing across the water. Observe the water's surface. Then try blowing very hard and keep blowing as long as you can. Observe the surface water now. Describe the changes in the water's surface from when you started the wind, after several minutes, and at different wind strengths.

To show that the form of the wave moves as energy, not water molecules, place a cork or ball on the water before you begin the experiment. Blow over the water to make waves, but be careful not to blow the ball. Observe that the wave will move by the ball but will not move it. The cork or ball will remain in the same spot.

OIL SPILL

Oil is lighter than water. It floats. After an oil spill, birds and marine mammals can become coated with oil from the water's surface and die. Likewise, much of their food becomes contaminated, and since oil is dark and shadows the water below, it prevents marine plants from receiving the light they need to grow.

When an oil spill comes ashore, it coats the beaches and marshes. This is harmful to the intertidal animals and plants, and unpleasant for the tourist.

Cleaning up oil spills is very costly and time consuming. Scientists are trying to develop better methods for containing oil spills. Here are some of the methods used now: 1) containing the oil spill with floating boundaries, then drawing oil and water from the ocean's surface; 2) using detergents to break down the oil; and 3) soaking up the oil with straw and other porous materials, then collecting the straw.

PURPOSE
To investigate methods for cleaning up an oil spill in water.

MATERIALS
A small amount of motor oil, a feather, detergent, cotton balls, and tray

PROCEDURE
In a tray of water, pour a teaspoon of motor oil. Note that the oil spreads and very little is needed. Dip your finger in the water to see how the oil coats. Sweep the surface with a feather. What happens?

Explore different ways to clean up the oil and evaluate the results. Try containing the oil with floating pencils or dissolving the oil with detergent. Also, try soaking up the oil with cotton or straw.

••

MAKE IT RAIN! WATER CYCLE IN A JAR!

You can make a miniature hydrologic cycle using very simple materials. Once you have tried the experiment, you may want to vary the materials by adding soil, small plants, shells, or rocks. Observe your mini-environment and record the events you see.

MATERIALS
An empty glass jar, cups, or aquarium, warm water, a piece of glass or heavy plastic wrap, a rubber band, ice cubes

PROCEDURE
Put several inches of warm water in the jar. Cover it immediately with a piece of glass or the plastic wrap that can be held tightly in place by the rubber band. Put several ice cubes on top of the glass or plastic wrap to simulate the cold air in the atmosphere. Place the jar in a sunny window or near a heat source. As the warm air from the water rises and meets the cold covering, what happens? Do you see clouds? Rain?

Science experiments used with permission of UNC Sea Grant, NOAA, US.

WHEN TWO PLATES MEET AND ONE IS FORCED UNDER THE OTHER, THIS IS CALLED A _____ ZONE.

_____ IS THE PROCESS OF USING THE SUN'S ENERGY TO PRODUCE FOOD.

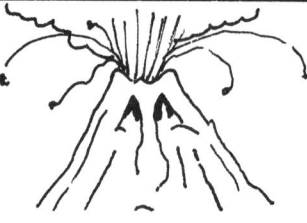

TRUE OR FALSE? VOLCANOES CAN ERUPT UNDER WATER AND FORM CONTINENTS.

TRUE OR FALSE? THE HEATED WATER FROM A THERMAL VENT IS RICH IN HYDROGEN SULFIDE GAS.

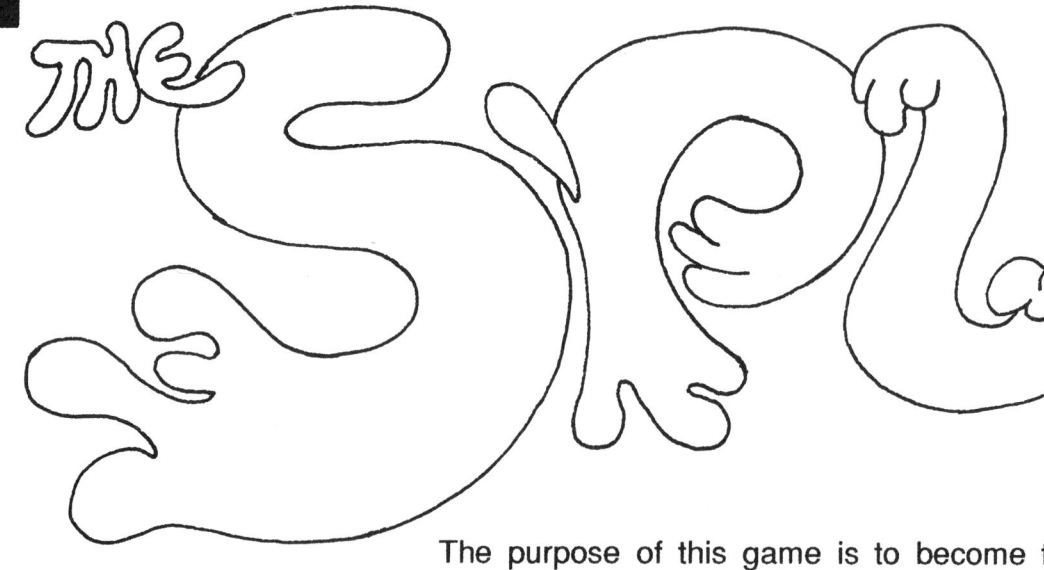

The purpose of this game is to become f... hydrologic phenomena found in the **OUR** ...

INSTRUCTIONS
Two or three players may participate. Each player needs a to... great!). Place the tokens on START space and begin the game ... player with the highest number goes first. Each player, in turn ... moves the token the number of spaces shown on the die. The ... answer the question in the space or return to his original positi... for his next turn. All answers can be found in the text of the bo... on a SPLASH space, the player removes the top SPLASH car... follows the directions. The first player to arrive at the FINISH ... Before you begin to play, cut apart the SPLASH cards found in th... EXTRA PAPER and place on the game board in the labeled sp...

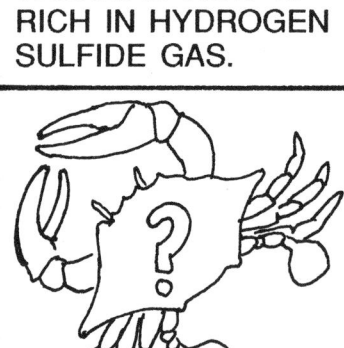

WHAT IS THE SCIENTIFIC NAME FOR THE SHELL OF A CRAB?

NAME THREE EXAMPLES OF BENTHIC LIFE.

SEAWEED RELEASES _____ DURING PHOTOSYNTHESIS.

A SCALLOP'S SHELL IS SECRETED BY THE _____.

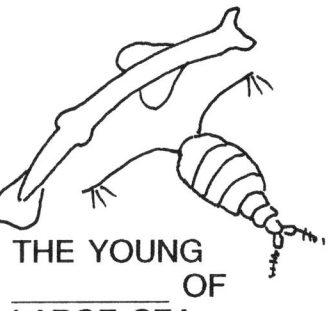
THE YOUNG _____ OF LARGE SEA ANIMALS, WHICH FEED ON PHYTOPLANKTON.

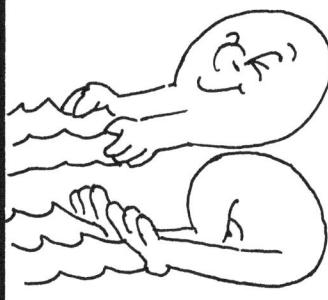
_____ RISE HIGHER AND FALL LOWER THAN OTHER TIDES.

...r with the geographic, geologic, and
...D: THE WATER PLANET.

...shells would be
...ssing a die. The
...ses the die and
...r must correctly
...d wait
...the token lands
...m the deck and
...e is the winner.
...yl bag with your

Copyright © 1992 Puppetools, Inc.

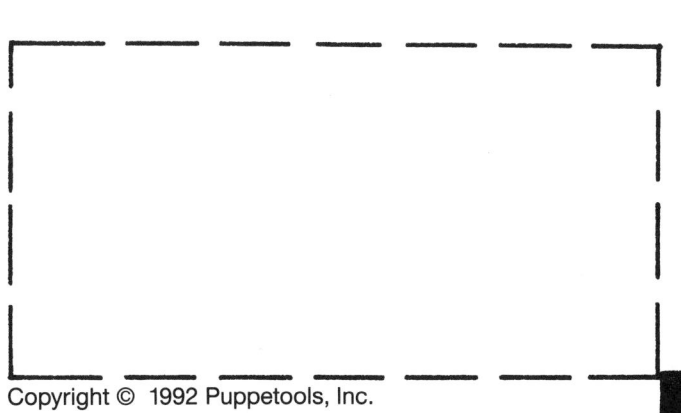

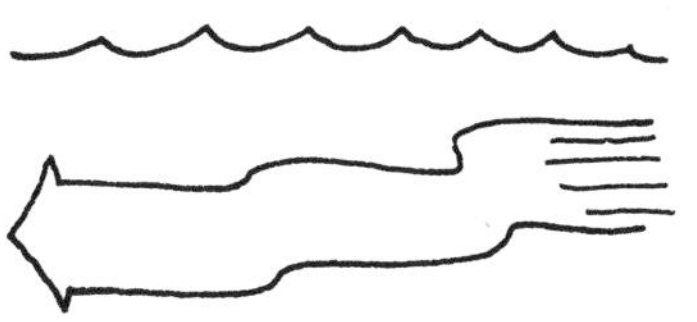

A CURRENT CAN BE COMPARED TO A _____ FLOWING THROUGH THE OCEAN.

TRUE OR FALSE? THE SEA STAR'S BRAIN IS LOCATED IN ITS CENTRAL DISK.

LIST THREE ANIMALS THAT ARE NECKTON.

DID YOU KNOW...

* There are many types of **SCIENTISTS** who study the oceans and the formation of the earth's surface. If you would like to know more about any of these exciting careers, you can research them in your library.

> METEOROLOGISTS study the phenomena of the atmosphere, weather, and weather conditions.
> BIOLOGISTS study life and life processes of the animal and plant kingdoms.
> MARINE BIOLOGISTS specialize in aquatic life forms.
> GEOLOGISTS study the origin, history, and physical structure of the planet as recorded through rocks and minerals.
> OCEANOGRAPHERS study the geography of the ocean and all its phenomenon.
> PALEONTOLOGISTS study fossils and ancient life forms in geologic periods.
> CHEMISTS study the composition, structure, and properties of elementary substances.
> PHYSICISTS study the properties of matter and energy and how they interact.
> SEISMOLOGISTS study earthquakes.

* In the eighteenth century, mail that was sent by ship took two weeks longer to make the transatlantic voyage than did merchant and fishing ships. **Benjamin Franklin**, the postmaster general, talked to a Nantucket whaling captain who had observed the mail ships riding the current rather than crossing it. Stemming the current took the ships much longer. Ben Franklin had a chart of the **Gulf Stream** prepared in 1769 to educate the captains of the mail ships. He used information gathered by Captain Timothy Folger, the whaler. Captain Folger's experience had taught him that whales gather on either side of the Gulf Stream. It is also possible that he may have used the contrast between the surface temperature and the current temperature to chart the flow of the stream.

* **Baleen whales** are the largest animals that live in the sea. The blue whale can grow to 100 feet long and can weigh up to 130 tons! These huge mammals feed on plankton. They do not have teeth to catch their food but are equipped with baleen plates which are suspended from their upper jaw. The whale takes water into its mouth as it swims. When the mouth is full, the whale closes its jaw and forces the water through the baleen plates. The baleen, which looks like a comb, strains krill (that resemble small shrimp) and other nourishment from the plankton. The food is then swallowed. An adult blue whale can eat up to four tons a day! The humpback whale "herds" large amounts of plankton together by blowing bubbles that serve as a net. It dives deep and begins to swim upward in a circular pattern, all the while blowing bubbles through its two blowholes. The net of bubbles keeps the plankton together and forces them to the surface where the baleen whale swims up with its jaws open and feeds on the large catch. Baleen whales' behavior indicate that they enjoy active play! They are acrobatic and can often be seen breaching (leaping out of and diving into the water) as many as twenty times in a row.

A LITTLE EXTRA INFORMATION

PANGAEA means "all the world." The single, large supercontinent began to break up about 200 million years ago into two large land masses, **GONDWANALAND and LAURASIA**. These later divided into the continents, which slowly drifted into the geographic locations that we now know. They are still drifting.

CONVECTION CURRENTS are currents caused by the movement of hot rocks rising within the mantle, cooling, then sinking back into the mantle. This continual motion causes the earth's rigid plates to move, carrying the oceans and continents with them.

An **ARCHIPELAGO** is a large group of islands.

EVAPORATION is the process of a substance going from liquid to gas by exposure to air or heat and being dispersed into the atmosphere. **EVAPO-TRANSPIRATION** is the process of water evaporating from plants. **CONDENSATION** is the process of a substance changing from gas to a liquid, usually from cooling. **PRECIPITATION** is the process by which moisture returns from the atmosphere to the land by rain, sleet, or snow.

GROUNDWATER is water stored naturally underground that comes to the surface in springs. The water seeps through the soil and settles between rock layers.

A TROPHIC PYRAMID is designed to show the relationship of food chains and to show the amount of food necessary to support the next level of life in the nutritive process. Only about 10% of the available energy is really used by the next group on the pyramid, so it takes ten times more of that food source to sustain the next level of life. (Example: 100 diatoms feed 10 little fish who then feed 1 crab).

PRODUCERS are organisms that make their own food by using the energy of the sun and are the base of the pyramid. Animals that feed directly on producers are called **HERBIVORES** or **PRIMARY CONSUMERS** and are the second level. Any organism that cannot produce its own food and eats other organisms for nourishment is a **CONSUMER**. If an animal eats both plants and animals, it is called an **OMNIVORE** or a **SECONDARY CONSUMER**. They are level three of the pyramid. At the top of the pyramid are animals that feed only on other animals, **CARNIVORES**. They are **PREDATORS** and are the last link in the food chain.

PHOTOSYNTHESIS is a chemical process by which green plants make carbohydrates from water and carbon dioxide using the sun's energy. Oxygen is a waste product.

DIATOMS are microscopic, single celled algae.

The science of **TAXONOMY** is a system used to classify life forms using shared characteristics. The largest divisions are called **KINGDOMS**. There are five of these divisions, but the two we refer to most often are the plant and animal kingdoms. The next level is the **PHYLUM**. Phylums are the major divisions within the kingdoms. A **CLASS** of organisms share the most similar traits or characteristics. The **SPECIES** is the most unique group that share the same set of structural traits and can successfully reproduce.

ENZYMES are proteins that speed up or modify a chemical reaction but are not altered in the process.

CREATE YOUR OWN UNDERSEA WORLD FOR YOUR PUPPET PALS!

It is your turn to be creative. Make a natural underwater environment for your puppets. Use the information in the book, look through the pictures for details, and think about how you envision an ideal habitat for your puppets. Sketch your ideas here.

Some possible backgrounds for building your undersea world could be a large bulletin board, a big box, or an old sheet. It might be fun to use modeling clay or papier mache' to form an ocean floor. Other materials that you can use for your model are the EXTRA PAPER in the back of the book, paint, markers, green or blue plastic film (like Saran Wrap), real shells, or other natural materials from the beach. Remember you can include seaweed and other plants and animals that are found in the sea.

Enlist your friends to help stage a rock or country music concert for your puppets to perform. Write your own music or lyrics to reflect life in the ocean. You can adapt familiar songs with your own lyrics. An example could be Home, Home on the Abyssal Plain...... or Crabby Crustacean to the tune of "Rocky Racoon". The show could have a master of ceremonies, a comedian, talent competitions, or people tricks (similar to pet tricks).

Your finished environment will be a great place to interact with your puppets or to stage plays. Try developing a story starter into a one-act play. Make extra props when you need them. You may even want to design a new puppet for your cast. Another idea is to conduct interviews with the puppets (maybe a "puppet-on-the-beach" interview) about some pollution solutions.

Try your hand at the world of advertising! Make up and stage your own commercials for products that your puppets' community might buy. An example might be a new improved super sponge for soaking up oil spills. Or the Gulf Stream could advertise its speedy, non-stop delivery from North America to Europe. A thermal vent could offer a warm, rejuvenating soak to cure the winter doldrums. Your puppets could even stage an awards show to pick the best advertising commercial of the year!

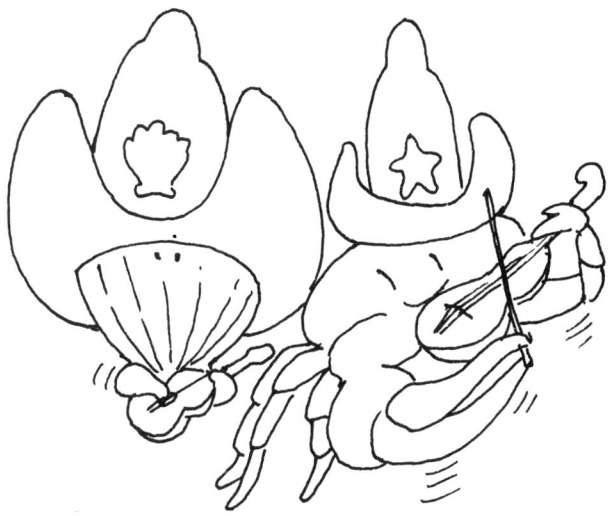

Pretend this is an election year in the ocean. Decide what the issues will be. Be certain that the issues are important to marine life, and therefore, important to all life. Let the candidates stage a debate or persuasive speeches. Make up catchy slogans and campaign banners. Hold a rally. Let your friends or family vote for the best candidate.

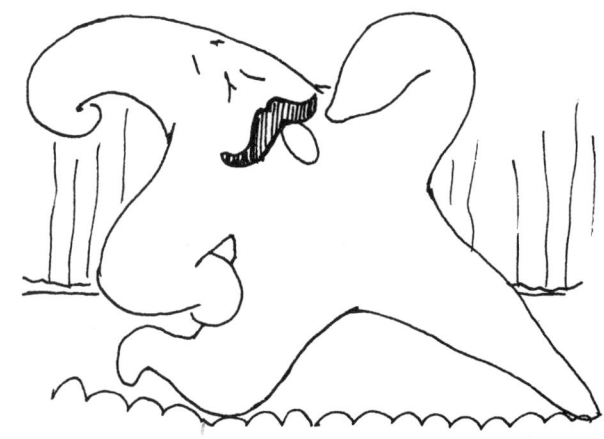

ABOUT YOUR PUPPETS

We know that animals cannot talk or reason. But for a sense of play, you can personify your puppets. Our products are designed to be **FUN-da-MENTAL**. They invite you to have fun while discovering exciting facts about oceanography, exploring some new ideas, thinking creatively, and playing with puppets. The activities provide a variety of avenues to tickle, challenge, tease, and entertain you and your friends. Below are some suggestions for enhancing the fun with your puppets:

-Experiment with a variety of voices to discover a personality for your puppets. Each puppet's voice should be easy to identify and listen to. A repeated line or pet phrase may become part of each puppet's speech pattern.

-Movement also contributes to and reflects the personality of each puppet. Practice moving your puppets from side to side, up and down, forward and back, in circles, wiggling, bending forward, as if walking, running, jumping, hiding, pointing, laughing. Twist your wrist to make the puppet turn its head from side to side, tilting it at different angles, forward and back, up and down. Move the puppet in natural tempo to see what it says.

-Through voice and movement, a personality develops. Add to your puppets' design to match their characters and personalize them. Use yarn, buttons, pipe cleaners, rick rack, and other scrap materials you may find.

-Practice interacting with the puppets, keeping each one in character. They could discuss some of the facts or activities in the book, or they could choose one of the story starters and tell a story round-robin, with each puppet adding to the story until it comes to a logical conclusion. The puppets might also engage in problem-solving, discussing some of the points to ponder or ecological problems posed in the book.

It is our hope that this book and the puppets will open the door to exploration of new worlds and communication between you and your friends. Have a good time as you discover **OUR EARTH: THE WATER PLANET** science fun!

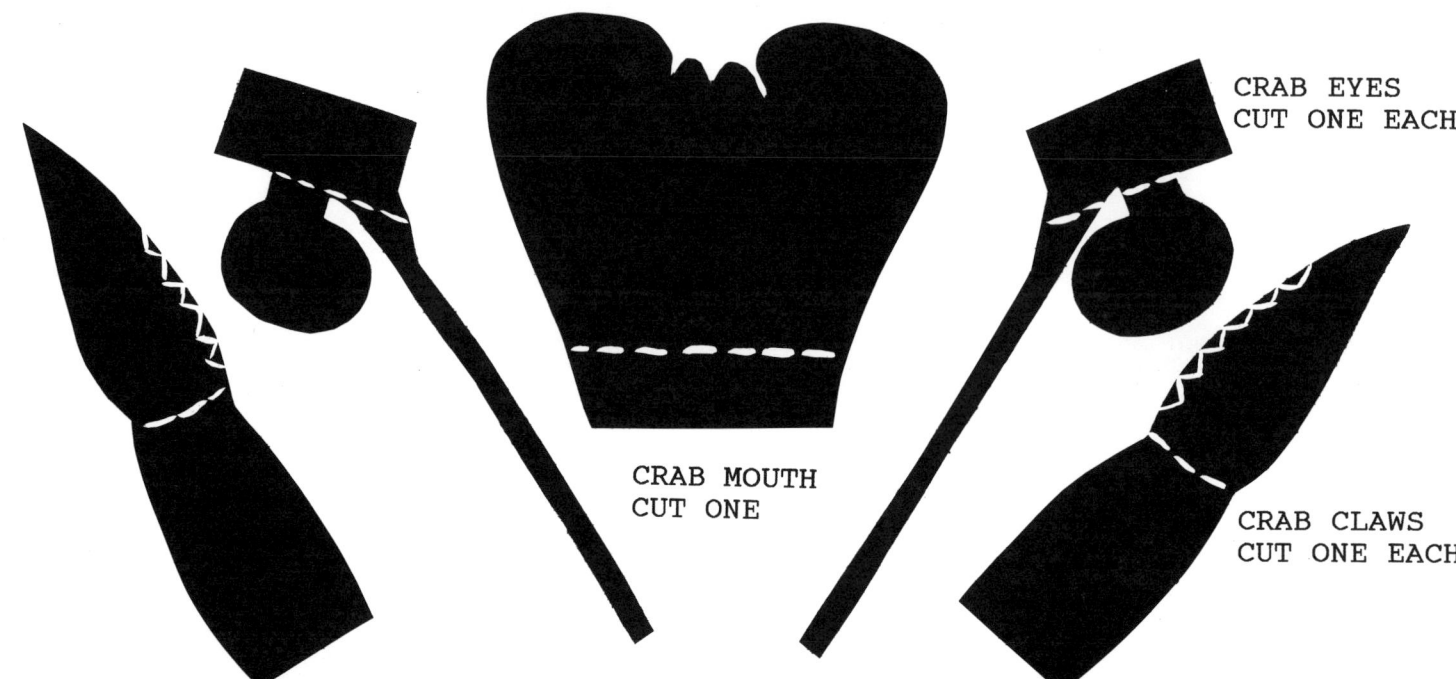

CRAB EYES
CUT ONE EACH

CRAB MOUTH
CUT ONE

CRAB CLAWS
CUT ONE EACH

PUPPET PATTERNS

"I work on a paper hinge like this. All my parts go together like a puzzle — a paper puzzle that really "talks."

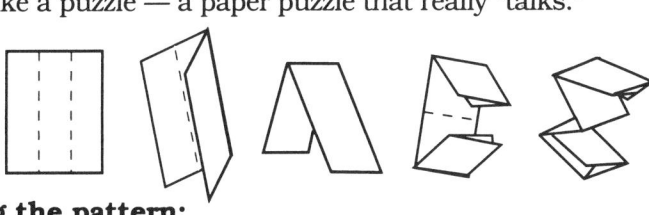

Using the pattern:
1. Cut out each pattern part.
2. Trace each pattern part onto construction paper. Use bright, contrasting colors for different parts. Remember there *are* such things as purple crabs.
3. Cut the parts from construction paper.
4. Attach puppet parts as shown.
5. Keep pattern parts in your puppet bag so you can make the puppet again.

Materials you'll need: glue-stic, scissors, markers, construction paper.

To make the Paper Talker® Hinge, fold a 6 x 9 inch piece of construction paper as shown above.

SCALLOP MANTLE
CUT TWO

SCALLOP EYES
CUT SIXTEEN

SCALLOP SHELL
CUT TWO

SCALLOP MUSCLE
CUT ONE

Paper Talker® U.S. Patent 4,555,236
©1989 Puppetools. All rights reserved.
P.O. Box 32000, Richmond, Virginia 23261

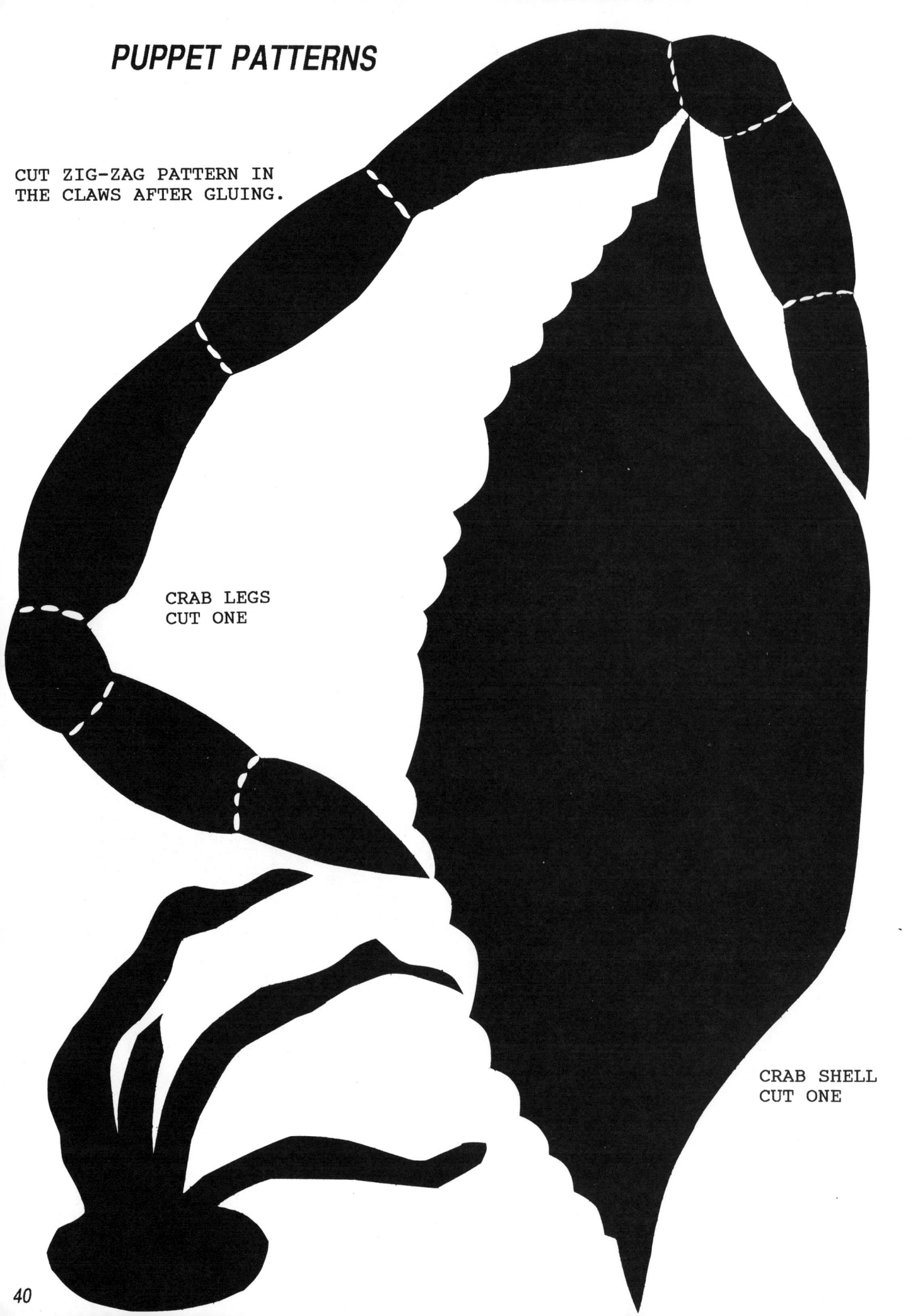

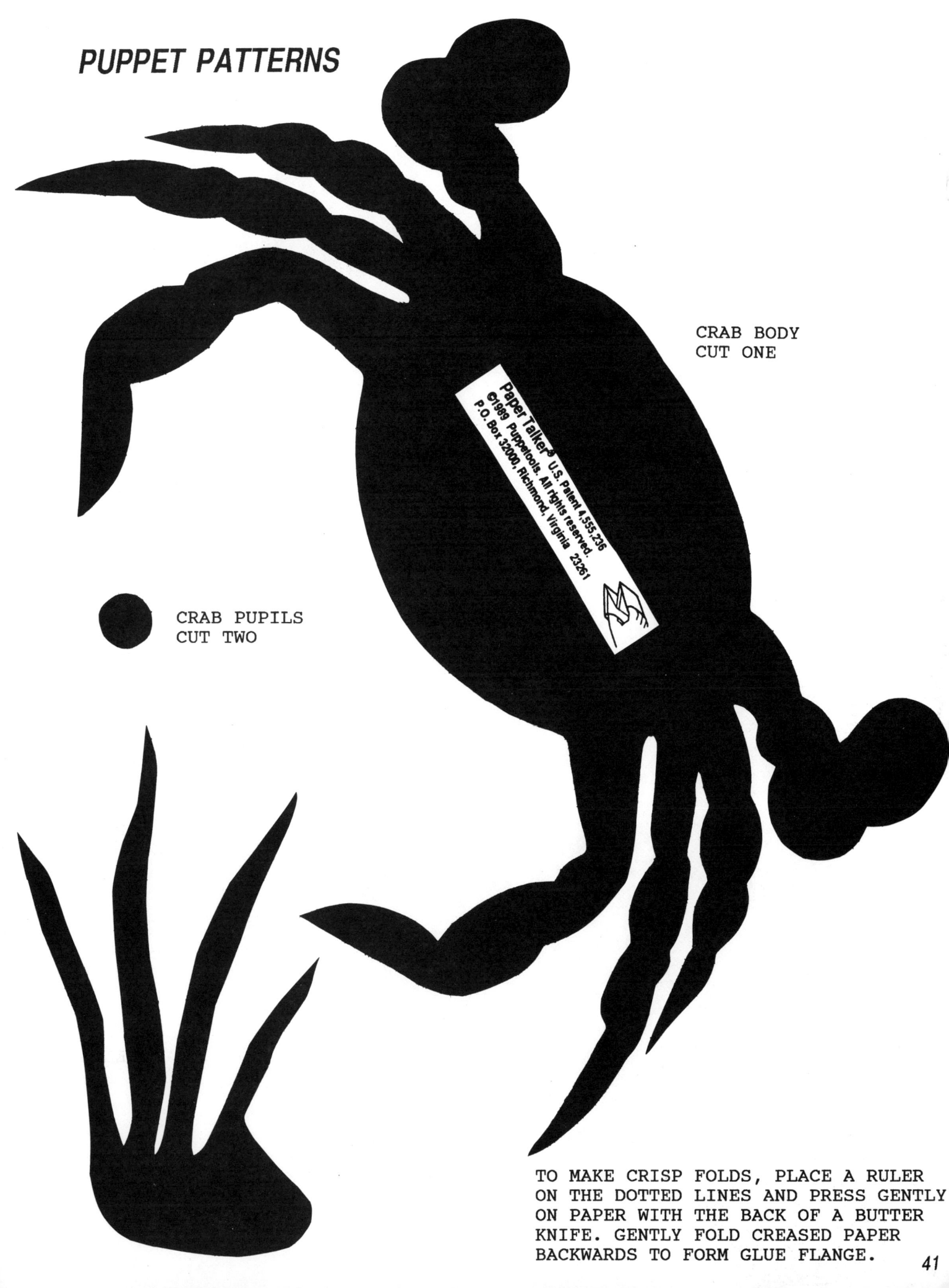

PUPPET PATTERNS

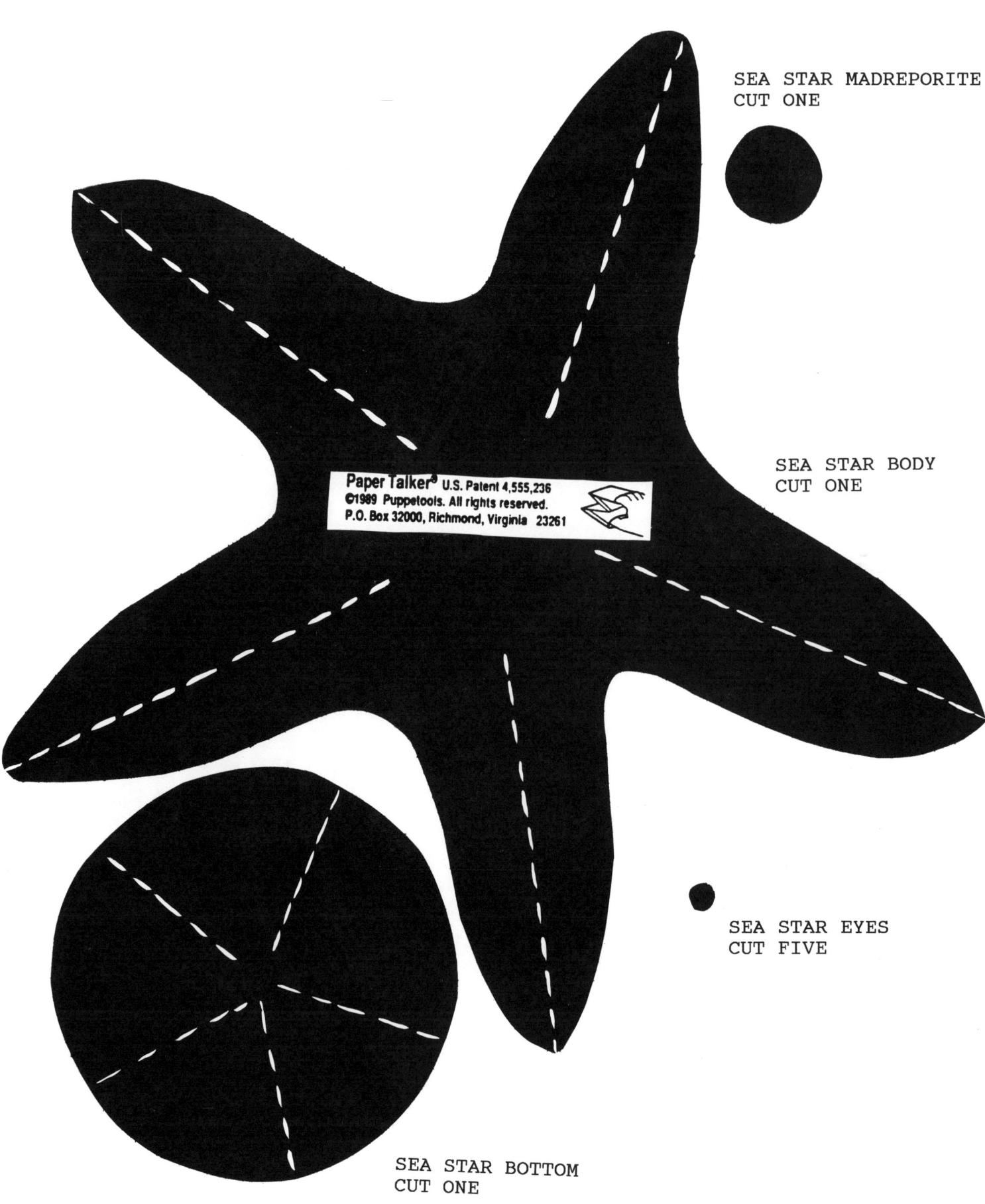

BIBLIOGRAPHY

FICTION

Andrews, Jan. **THE VERY LAST FIRST TIME.** Macmillan, 1986.
Bowdan, Joan Chase. **WHY THE TIDES EBB AND FLOW.** Houghton Mifflin, 1979.
Buck, Pearl. **THE BIG WAVE.** Harper and Row, 1947.
Cole, Joanna. **THE MAGIC SCHOOL BUS AT THE WATERWORKS.** Scholastic, 1986.
Cole, Joanna. **THE MAGIC SCHOOL BUS ON THE OCEAN FLOOR.** Scholastic, 1992.
Coony, Barbara. **ISLAND BOY.** Viking Penguin, 1988.
Holling, Holling C. **PADDLE TO THE SEA.** Houghton Mifflin, 1941.
Holling, Holling C. **PAGOO.** Houghton Mifflin, 1957.
Holling, Holling C. **SEABIRD.** Houghton Mifflin, 1948.
Kipling, Rudyard. **THE JUST SO STORIES.** Doubleday, 1912, 1952.
O'Dell, Scott. **ISLAND OF THE BLUE DOLPHINS.** Dell, 1987.
Roop, Connie and Peter. **KEEP THE LIGHTS BURNING, ABBIE.** Down East Press, 1969.
Shannon, George. **SEA GIFTS.** David R. Godine, 1989.
Taylor, Theodore. **THE CAY.** Avon Books, 1969.

NONFICTION

Asimov, Isaac. **HOW DID WE FIND OUT ABOUT LIFE IN THE DEEP SEA?** Avon Books, 1982.
Carson, Rachel. **THE EDGE OF THE SEA.** Houghton Mifflin, 1955.
Center for Marine Conservation. **THE OCEAN BOOK.** John Wiley & Son, 1989.
Chinery, Michael. **OCEAN ANIMALS.** Random House, 1992.
Coulombe, Deborah A. **THE SEASIDE NATURALIST, A GUIDE TO STUDY AT THE SEASHORE.** Prentice Hall Press, 1984.
Feeny, Stephanie and Feilding, Ann. **SAND TO SEA.** University of Hawaii Press, 1989.
Griggs, Tamar. **THERE'S A SOUND IN THE SEA: A CHILD'S EYE VIEW OF A WHALE.** Scrimshaw, 1975.
Lindbergh, Anne Morrow. **GIFT FROM THE SEA.** Pantheon, 1975.
Malnig, Anita. **WHERE THE WAVES BREAK: LIFE AT THE EDGE OF THE SEA.** Carolrhoda Books, 1985.
McGovern, Ann. **SHARK LADY, TRUE ADVENTURES OF EUGENIA CLARK.** Scholastic Book Services, 1978.
Nieson, Thomas M. **THE MARINE BIOLOGY COLORING BOOK.** Harper Perennial, 1982.
Robinson, W. Wright. **INCREDIBLE FACTS ABOUT THE OCEAN (Vols. 1,2).** Dillon Press, 1987.
Sibbald, Jean H. **SEA CREATURES ON THE MOVE.** Dillon Press, 1986.
Wells, Susan. **THE ILLUSTRATED WORLD OCEANS.** Simon & Schuster, 1991.

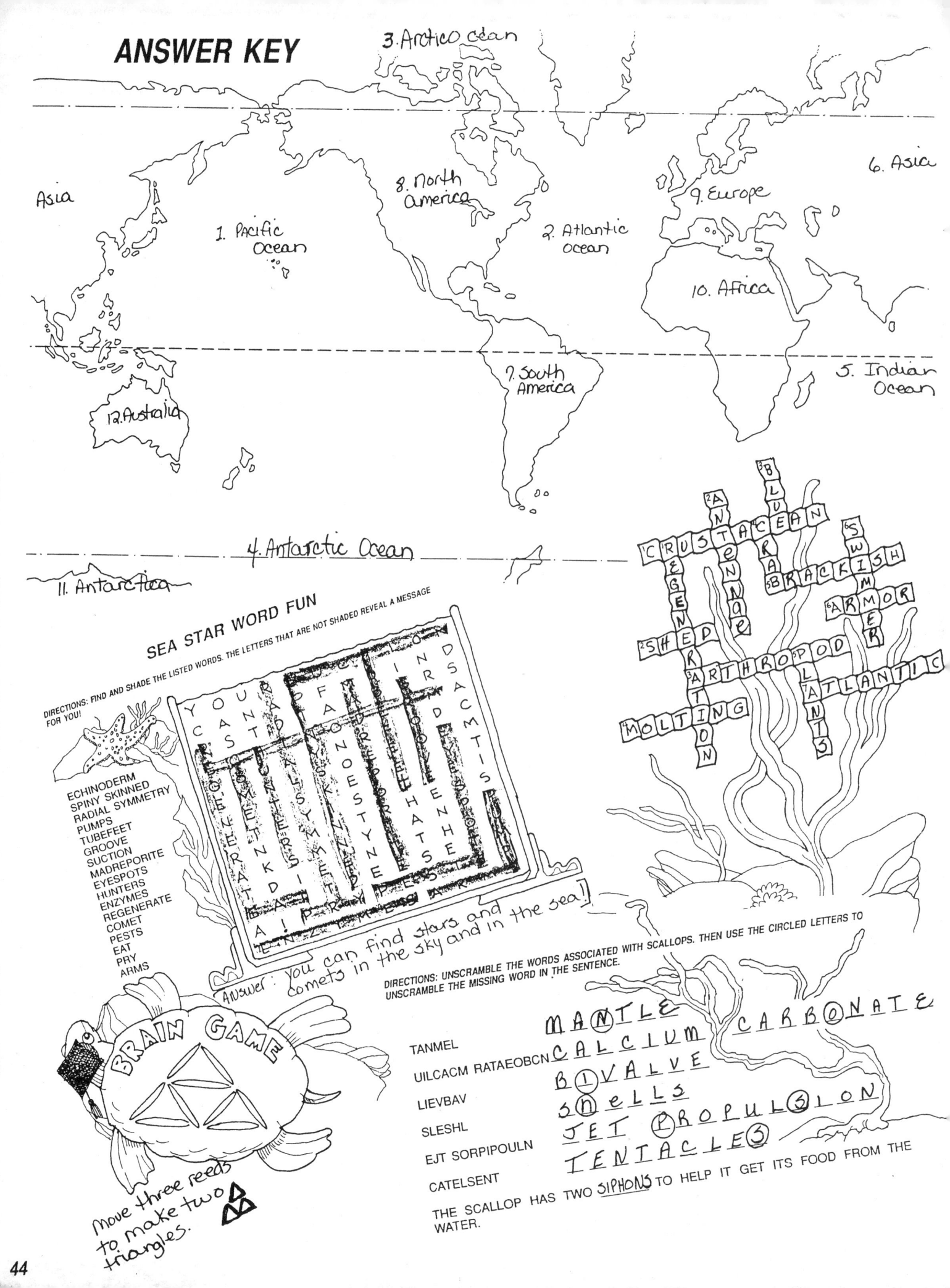